A must-have for all knitters who want to better understand lace—and the diverse knitting world!

> Annie Modesitt
> Author of *Twist & Loop* (Potter Craft) and *Men Who Knit and the Dogs Who Love Them* (Lark Books)

Arctic Lace is most comprehensive, highly creative, and wonderfully detailed. The lace designs inspired by Native Alaskan art are unique treasures certain to appeal to any knitter!

> Ann McCauley
> Author of *The Pleasures of Knitting* (Martingale & Company)

From the rich, historic background of the indigenous Alaskan-American peoples comes the art form of beautiful lace fashioned from the wool of the musk ox. The wealth of patterns included in the book make it equally valuable to the beginner, intermediate, or advanced lace knitter. The easy 1–2–3 tutorials, detailed stitch library, and handy templates aid us in indulging our knitting passion and designing our own lace projects.

> Marcia Lewandowski
> Author of *Folk Mittens* (Interweave Press) and *Andean Folk Knits* (Lark Books)

Donna is at it again, doing what she does best—giving us a hands-on, in-depth look at historical knitting and modernizing it for the knitter who needs to know.

> Cheryl Potter
> Author of *Lavish Lace* (Martingale & Company)

I have been involved with Oomingmak Musk Ox Producers' Co-operative since 1969 and have longed to see the history and story of this unusual co-operative written down. I think that *Arctic Lace* will help to introduce more people to a truly luxurious fiber, to some of Alaska's peoples, and to these remnants of the last Ice Age, the musk ox. I am pleased to see that Donna has helped to capture the spirit of the co-op and is honoring the resilient knitting members of the co-op.

> Sigrun Robertson
> Executive Director, Oomingmak Musk Ox Producers' Co-operative

Arctic Lace

Arctic Lace

Knitting Projects and Stories Inspired by Alaska's Native Knitters

Donna Druchunas

NOMAD PRESS FORT COLLINS, COLORADO

To the knitters of Oomingmak

Cover design: Mayapriya Long / Bookwrights
Cover inset image: Oomingmak Musk Ox Producers' Co-operative members and knitters Mesonga Atkinson, Margaret Hobbs, Eliza Tom, and Joyce Haynes / Photo by Chris Arend, courtesy of Chris Arend and Oomingmak Musk Ox Producers' Co-operative
Cover background image: Lace stole / Photo by Dominic Cotignola
Interior design: Deborah Robson
Photographs: Dominic Cotignola, unless otherwise credited
Copyediting, proofreading, and index: Kathryn Banks, Eagle-Eye Indexing
Illustrations: Gayle Ford

Printed in Canada

Publisher's Cataloging-in-Publication
(Provided by Quality Books, Inc.)

Druchunas, Donna.
    Arctic lace : knitting projects and stories inspired by Alaska's native knitters / Donna Druchunas.
    p. cm.
    Includes bibliographical references and index.
    LCCN 2006920805
    ISBN-13: 978-0-9668289-7-9
    ISBN-10: 0-9668289-7-6
    1. Knitted lace—Alaska—Patterns. 2. Eskimos—Alaska—Social life and customs. 3. Eskimo business enterprises—Alaska. 4. Oomingmak Musk Ox Producers o-operative. I. Title.

TT805.K54D78 2006   746.2'26041
                QBI06–600312

A number of quotations in chapter 2, individually indicated, are reprinted from *Authentic Alaska: Voices of Its Native Writers* by Susan B. Andrews and John Creed by permission of the University of Nebraska Press. Copyright © 1998 by the University of Nebraska Press. Other permissions are credited within the text.

The fonts used to compose the charts in this book were designed by David Xenakis, who has generously made them available for use by other knitters and designers in both amateur and professional capacities, as long as their source is credited—which we are delighted to do. This is an enormous service to the knitting community. Knitter's Symbols fonts used courtesy *Knitter's Magazine*—Copyright © 1998 XRX, Inc.

Text fonts are Usherwood, Avocet, Laricio, and Myriad.

Nomad Press proudly participates in the Green Press Initiative, which works to create paper-use transformations that conserve natural resources and preserve endangered resources.

www.greenpressinitiative.org

Nomad Press contributes a percentage of its resources to non-profit organizations working on projects related to the topics of its books. In addition, a percentage of the author's royalties are being donated to Oomingmak Musk Ox Producers' Co-operative.

Printing by Friesens   10 9 8 7 6

Nomad Press
PO Box 484
Fort Collins CO 80522-0484
www.nomad-press.com

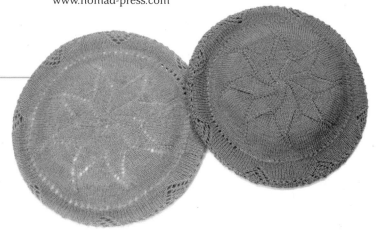

North Star Tam knitted in lace-weight qiviut (left) and fingering-weight wool (right). Both laces are successful, although the body, stitch definition, and softness of the fabrics vary.

Contents

Dominic Cotignola

I was driven to find out as much as I could about the Native American women who knit this mystery fiber, qiviut, into lace. My quest took me to the Internet, to the library, to conversations with yarn companies in Canada, and ultimately to Alaska, where I finally found Oomingmak—"the bearded one" in the Inupiat language.

Following my obsessions to the Arctic

*P*icture yourself surrounded by the softest fiber you can imagine. Skeins of yarn, tufts of fleece, delicate knitted lace envelop you. The nearly weightless fiber has the texture of a cloud. The yarn is fine and fluffy, with a hand that reminds you of a kitten's fur. The lace drapes like fine-woven silk. As you touch the lace scarves—in natural taupe and soft, muted colors—you notice a gentle halo lightly framing the stitches, adding a dimension of luxury not quite like anything you've ever seen. Softer than merino, finer than cashmere, lighter than silk, the fiber you are touching is qiviut, the down of the musk ox.

I first learned about qiviut in an article in *PieceWork* magazine in 1996. Janet Catherine Berlo told of visiting a group of Native Alaskan women who knit with this incredible fiber.[1] The article drew me in. I was driven to find out as much as I could about these women and this mystery fiber they were knitting into lace. Thus began the adventure that led to this book. My quest took me to the Internet, to the library, to conversations with yarn companies in Canada, and ultimately to Alaska, where I finally found Oomingmak ("the bearded one" in the Inupiat language).

Approximately two hundred Native Alaskan women from remote coastal villages of Alaska own and operate Oomingmak Musk Ox Producers' Co-operative. Using yarn spun from musk ox down, these artisans hand-knit intricate lace items. Each village has a signature stitch pattern derived from Eskimo culture. Lacy images of harpoons, native dancers, and butterflies—inspired by ancient artifacts and beadwork designs—decorate scarves, nachaqs (hoods), and caps. The co-op store, located in Anchorage, sells these items

Opposite: Meeting a baby musk ox at the Musk Ox Farm in Palmer, Alaska.

---

[1] Janet Catherine Berlo, "Oomingmak: Knitting Vision into Reality," *PieceWork* 4, no. 1 (January/February 1996): 50.

to supplement the resources of the knitters so they can maintain their traditional lifestyles.

Dorothy Reade, a pioneer in the use of knitting charts, developed a three-step technique for teaching lace knitting. In the 1960s, she taught the elegant lace-knitting techniques used by the co-op knitters to the co-op's founders. In December 1968, the co-op sent Ann Lillian Schell to the village of Mekoryuk to teach the first members how to follow charts and how to work with lace-weight qiviut yarn.

Qiviut is harvested from musk oxen in the wild and on farms. The first musk ox farm, started in 1956, still provides qiviut fiber to the co-op. Some fiber is also harvested from animals taken in Inuit hunts in Canada. (Although musk oxen were once extinct in Alaska and their numbers were greatly reduced in Canada, today there are over 150,000 animals in the wild.)

During my stay in Alaska, I was privileged to visit the Oomingmak store, the Musk Ox Farm, and one Eskimo village, and to meet several of the co-op's expert knitters. I also visited museums, cultural centers, and bookstores in my quest to learn about the knitters' cultures and history.

In *Arctic Lace*, I invite you to join me on my journey in learning about the extraordinary knitters, unusual animals, luxurious fiber, and beautiful lace knitting of Oomingmak.

The opening chapters of this book paint a picture of life in rural Alaska. In these chapters, you will learn about the rich cultures of the Yup'ik and Inupiat peoples as well as the history of the Musk Ox Farm and of Oomingmak Musk Ox Producers' Co-operative.

Who are the Eskimos?

Before I went to Alaska, I thought it was disrespectful to use the term Eskimo. When I arrived, however, I saw and heard the word used everywhere I went, including by Native Alaskans.

I was confused but soon discovered that there are many groups of Native Alaskan peoples. Both Yup'ik and Inupiat cultures are considered Eskimo, and the term is used when referring to both groups together. When referring to one group individually, Yup'ik or Inupiat is preferred.

In Canada and Greenland, the term Inuit is used instead of Eskimo to refer to the people closely related to the Alaskan Inupiats.

See Chapter 2 for more information on Native Alaskan peoples.

Chapters 6 and 7 include information about working with qiviut yarn, instructions for reading and knitting from lace charts, and a three-step tutorial that will give you the confidence and skill to knit the projects. Because qiviut is one of the most expensive fibers available and you may want to practice with something else, I also provide tips for working with other lovely lace-weight yarns.

In preparing the designs for this book, I was inspired by Yup'ik and Inupiat art and culture. None of the designs in Chapter 8 is a traditional Oomingmak pattern; to obtain the real thing, you will want to contact the co-op. The designs of the Oomingmak co-op are copyrighted, and the income generated by the knitters through working these designs supplements their subsistence lifestyles.

By working one or more of the patterns I have designed for you, however, I hope that you will gain a deep appreciation for the traditional designs while increasing your own knitting skills. From very easy wrist warmers to an intricate vest and shawl, there is something here to help knitters at every skill level understand the accomplishments of the Oomingmak knitters.

Whether you are new to knitting or a seasoned knitter, once you know the basic lace-knitting techniques, you'll be ready to design your own projects. In Chapter 9, you will find a stitch library and basic pattern templates to help you start creating your own original designs.

> The policy of Oomingmak Musk Ox Producers' Co-operative is to protect the privacy of its members. Therefore, with the exception of those who have given me express permission to use their names, I have changed the names of the knitters in this book.

I hope you will enjoy traveling with me through rural Alaska, meeting the people who have inhabited this land for millennia, exploring the habitat of the ancient musk ox who provides us with one of the world's softest and most luxurious fibers, and learning about lace knitting.

The home of Oomingmak Musk Ox Producers' Co-operative at the corner of 6th and H streets in downtown Anchorage.

Chapter 1

Oomingmak Musk Ox Producers' Co-operative

Although not obvious from its name, Oomingmak Musk Ox Producers' Co-operative is a co-op for Native Alaskan knitters. The co-op inhabits a small building at the corner of 6th and H streets in downtown Anchorage; this is where my quest to understand qiviut and the lace-knitting traditions of Alaska began. The first musk oxen I saw on my trip graze in brightly colored paint on the sides of the building; like their living counterparts in the wild, they are not intimidated by cold, snow, or long, dark winters. Although the building is small, the co-operative's story extends to small villages located across the state. It began over fifty years ago with a vision of a cottage industry that would provide income to hundreds of Native Alaskan women.

I arrived in Anchorage to visit the Oomingmak Co-op store before the start of the tourist season, which gave me the opportunity and privilege to meet and spend time with several knitters and with the staff. With the long days of summer come crowds of tourists and no opportunity to visit with the busy staff.

My husband and I flew into Anchorage on a Sunday when the store was closed. We drove downtown to find the store so we wouldn't be late for our appointment on Monday. On my first view of the co-op building, it seemed to me hardly adequate to contain a business that ties Alaskan villages to customers around the world. And yet the co-op has given a measure of economic self-sufficiency to the roughly two hundred knitters who now participate in its activities and all of the knitters who have gone before them.

The next morning, when I went into the small building, I found a store, a museum, an office, a library, and a workroom filling every inch of space. The atmosphere was warm, cozy, and comfortable. Shelves overflowed with knitted lace; the walls were covered with photographs of knitters, musk oxen, and celebrity

Dominic Cotignola

The co-op's building in Anchorage compactly houses a store, a museum, an office, a library, and a workroom.

visitors; the restroom/library was full of books; and the back office was crammed with computers, files, yarn, and packages.

On a typical day, four or five women staff the shop. They spend their days helping customers, answering the phone and e-mail, and washing and blocking scarves and nachaqs. During the off-season, the pace is slow and days are quiet. During

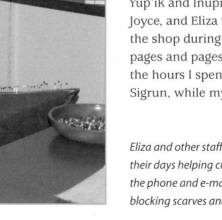

Dominic Cotignola

tourist season, the store is a flurry of activity from opening to closing, especially on sunny weekend afternoons.

Sigrun Robertson, the store's manager, is a feisty Swede. The rest of the staff members are reserved Yup'ik and Inupiat women. Marie, Joyce, and Eliza were working in the shop during my visit. I have pages and pages of notes from the hours I spent talking with Sigrun, while my husband took

Eliza and other staff members spend their days helping customers, answering the phone and e-mail, and washing and blocking scarves and nachaqs.

photographs and Marie kept the office and store running smoothly. I also sat with Joyce and Eliza for a couple of hours as they blocked nachaqs and scarves. We spoke—slowly and occasionally—about family, knitting, sewing, and the weather. Joyce has lived in Anchorage for twelve years, Eliza for even longer. Their families still live in the villages where they were born. Eliza's mother is seventy-eight and her father recently passed away at the same age. This was a leap year, and Eliza said her mother believes that every leap-year winter lasts longer than usual—a four-year peak of cold and snow. Both Joyce and Eliza speak in low, steady voices, without any urgency or attention-grabbing volume. They are also both expert knitters. Joyce knits Continental-style and Eliza knits English-style. Joyce can knit a nachaq in two nights: after work the first night, she casts on and knits one pattern repeat; the next night she completes the second repeat and binds off. Joyce prefers knitting nachaqs to scarves because they are knitted in the round and she doesn't have to purl. She can also knit a lace blanket in two weeks! These blankets aren't normally sold by the co-op, but the group raffles one off occasionally.

Most of the knitters in the co-op live on the Yukon-Kuskokwim Delta. Knitting comes naturally to the women of this region because they have artisan heritages that are centuries old. Even

Joyce prefers knitting nachaqs to scarves because they are knitted in the round and she doesn't have to slow down to purl.

Dominic Cotignola

Oomingmak Co-op products: Original lace work in pure qiviut

Nelson Island Nightmute nachaq.

The Musk Ox Producers' Co-operative sells two lines of qiviut accessories. The original line, developed in the 1960s when the co-op was first established, includes lace scarves, caps, hoods, and tunics made from 100 percent qiviut yarn. The lace knitting of the original line provided my inspiration for the projects in this book. It reflects the knitters' culture and is very different from patterns found anywhere else.

Nelson Island Nightmute scarf.

Photos of people by Chris Arend, courtesy of Chris Arend and Oomingmak Musk Ox Producers' Co-operative. Photo left by Dominic Cotignola.

before the arrival of the Russians in Alaska, Yup'ik and Inupiat women were highly skilled seamstresses and artists. They used their talents to sew fur clothing to protect their families from the elements and to weave baskets and even socks from grasses that grew in the region. Today, the women of the Yukon-Kuskokwim Delta are known as the finest basket weavers in Alaska.

The villages on this remote stretch of tundra are far away from oil fields and mines. There are few jobs, and even seasonal work is scarce. Men take most of the commercial fishing jobs. A few women work at the libraries, post offices, schools, and other government offices. In villages on the North Slope, there are more jobs and most women would choose the salary of a lucrative nine-to-five position over the small amounts earned knitting scarves and hats. However, knitting provides an opportunity to earn money for those who can't take full-time jobs. Because a knitting bag with a ball of qiviut yarn and two needles is small and lightweight, women can easily take their work along when they travel to fish camps and they can work on their projects while watching young

Oomingmak Co-op products: Tundra and Snow two-color work in qiviut/silk

The new line of products at Oomingmak, called Tundra and Snow, is knitted from a qiviut/silk blend and includes hats and headbands of stranded two-color knitting. Many of the Tundra and Snow designs are similar to Scandinavian color-knitting patterns. The Tundra and Snow items are knitted with qiviut purchased from the native people of Nunavut, Canada.

Left to right: Cloche, baby cap, and sunburst cap.

Photos by Chris Arend, courtesy of Chris Arend and Oomingmak Musk Ox Producers' Co-operative.

Knitting from charts

The lace patterns of Oomingmak are knitted by combining a few simple stitches that beginning knitters can learn with practice. Because many of the original co-op knitters did not speak English, the patterns are charted with symbols. Each symbol looks like the stitch it represents, and a co-op knitter will often have memorized a chart after making a few items in the signature pattern of her village.

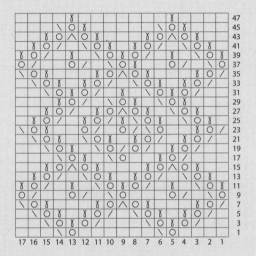

For information on how to read lace charts, see pages 95 to 98 and 181.

children. When getting a day job would be impractical or even impossible, knitting provides the ability to make money from a portable, interruptible craft.

Knitters join the co-op for many reasons. High school and college students may need money for weekend activities with their friends. Wives and mothers may want to supplement household income or purchase a specific item, such as a fishing boat or a new stove. If a woman needs money for a boat, she will knit until she has enough to make the purchase. Then she will take a break from knitting to focus on other areas of her life.

Today, some knitters have moved to Anchorage and can visit the store to turn in finished items and pick up yarn. Although they live in Anchorage, they still knit the patterns of their home villages. Those who live outside Anchorage correspond with the co-op primarily by mail. They receive yarn by mail, send back finished items, and receive more yarn along with their payment.

At the shop, the staff members examine each item received from the knitters and expertly fix the occasional dropped stitch or other mistake. They gently handwash the items and let them soak in clean water until they are saturated. Then they squeeze out the excess water, put a pile of scarves or nachaqs on the table, and start blocking.

Each member of the Oomingmak Co-op pays a $2 annual membership fee. Members do not pay for yarn; it is provided at the co-op's expense. This makes the co-op more profitable for members than other artists' co-ops in which members purchase their own supplies.

Dominic Cotignola

Not all of the knitters in Oomingmak knit to the same gauge, of course, so the items sent to Anchorage for blocking and sale are different sizes. The staff members in the store know exactly which knitters knit with loose, medium, or tight gauges, and automatically mark the sizes as large, medium, or small.

Oomingmak pays knitters by the stitch. Each project has a specific number of stitches cast on and a specific number of rows to knit, so the total can be easily calculated. The actual price per stitch changes with inflation, but the goal is to give the knitters a fair price while keeping the cost of the finished items reasonable. Still, the items are not inexpensive; handmade of a rare fiber, they are unique and precious.

At the end of the year, the profits of the co-op are distributed as dividends to the knitters, with each receiving a percentage based on the number of items knitted during the year.

When a village joins the co-op, the new knitters are treated to a workshop with Sigrun and an experienced co-op member. At this workshop, they learn how the co-op operates and how to knit the unique lace and natural color-work patterns. Each knitter makes several swatches to learn the techniques and to submit for evaluation before she is accepted into the co-op. While the techniques used are easy enough for new knitters to learn, experience is necessary to maintain the high quality necessary for items that will be sold.

If a new member joins from a village that already has a community of knitters, she receives a kit from the co-op with instructions on knitting a sample swatch that she will submit by mail for evaluation. She can work with other knitters in her village to learn any unfamiliar techniques.

Although the co-op products must be knitted from specific patterns, they can be knitted using any standard technique. Each co-op member knits in her own way. Some use the Continental method, others use the English method, and some even use the Eastern uncrossed method.

After spending a day in the Oomingmak store, I was curious about the origins of the soft fiber used to make their luxurious products. Luckily, I had two whole weeks to travel around Alaska following the trail of qiviut.

While I was visiting the shop, an older knitter came in to drop off some finished items and pick up more yarn. "I will never leave Alaska," she proclaimed loudly.

A recent trip to Utah convinced her: "They have no wild berries, only useless flowers." At ninety, she sounded ready to strike off to a new land if they did have berries!

The Musk Ox Farm

The day after I visited the Oomingmak store, I drove fifty minutes to Palmer to see a herd of musk oxen at the Musk Ox Farm. A sister organization to Oomingmak, the farm is the main supplier of qiviut to the co-op. Musk oxen are newcomers here, arriving only in 1989. The prehistoric-looking musk oxen seem slightly out of place in the quiet Matanuska Valley. Cows, pigs, and goats seem more at home among the traditional barns and farmhouses scattered across Alaska's agricultural center. Although musk oxen are native to Alaska, their natural range is far north of Anchorage and Palmer.

During tourist season, the farm provides educational tours to thousands of visitors. A typical summer may bring 25,000 visitors to the farm, making it one of the top three tourist destinations in Alaska. In 1994 when *Good Morning America* brought the

The Musk Ox Farm, in Palmer, is about forty miles northeast of Anchorage.

Adult musk ox at the Musk Ox Farm.

Musk Ox Farm into the living rooms of America, more than 35,000 visitors traveled to Alaska to see the animals face-to-face. In the off-season, the place is quiet. When they are not being herded into the barn for their weekly weighing and check-up, the musk oxen leisurely explore their pens and play with toys (street sweeper brushes, tires, and giant balls) and snacks (willow branches and pumpkins) scattered around their enclosures in an effort to keep them from getting bored and trying to escape.

Every spring, the co-op waits anxiously to find out how much qiviut has been combed from the animals. The farm has about forty animals, but the bulls and bred cows are not combed. Each animal sheds 5 to 6 pounds (2.3 to 2.7 kg) of qiviut a year, and the annual yield is only about 100 pounds (45 kg) of fiber. This sounds like a lot of fiber, considering that just 1 ounce (about 28 g) of finished qiviut yarn will make a lace nachaq. But the qiviut is cleaned and spun into yarn at a cashmere mill that will only process batches containing at least 600 pounds (272 kg), so it can take several years for the co-op to collect enough fiber for processing. In addition, about thirty percent of the fiber is lost during processing. It is a constant balancing act to make sure enough yarn is available to the knitters to keep up with customer demand.

Photos by Dominic Cotignola

19

The cultures of Alaskan Eskimos are complex, and I can only provide a small taste of their richness here.

Even amid modern changes, Yup'ik and Inupiat communities in Alaska have kept the traditions, languages, and art of their people alive.

Photo © Alaska Division of Tourism. Used by permission.

Chapter 2

The Yup'ik and Inupiat people

Visiting the retail shop in Anchorage and the Musk Ox Farm in Palmer gave me the opportunity to learn about the knitting and fiber of Oomingmak Musk Ox Producers' Co-operative. I also wanted to learn about the history and traditional culture of the Native peoples of Alaska. What better place than the museums and cultural centers around the state? Because I'm an avid reader, I also stopped at every bookstore I encountered and discovered more new and used books about Alaska than I thought possible. In each place I visited, I learned more and was increasingly intrigued by what I discovered.

I share with the knitters of Oomingmak a love of knitting, a passion for fine fibers, and an appreciation for traditions of the past. Before I was born, my Lithuanian and Russian family had assimilated into American culture. I don't speak the language of my grandparents and their parents, and I know very little about their traditions and values. Sadly, the only mementos I have of my origins are a few faded photographs and tattered recipes.

The Yup'ik and Inupiat people are no longer completely separate from Western influences after more than a century of contact—desired and undesired—with Russians, Europeans, and other Outsiders, but, even after a century of change, their cultural heritage is still largely intact.

To me, the story of the Oomingmak knitters is the story of the Yup'ik and Inupiat women, their villages, and their art. The cultures of Alaskan Eskimos are complex, and I can only provide a small taste of their richness here. In each section of this chapter, Eskimo speakers tell the stories of their own people. Some of the stories are traditional tales, others are contemporary writings.

Native peoples of Alaska

Over time, historians and anthropologists have developed many theories about the origins of Native Americans, and of Eskimos in particular. These theories range from bizarre and preposterous to credible and scientific. Some early explorers surmised that these first Alaskans were a lost tribe of Israel. Others claimed that the Eskimos came from a utopian civilization hidden deep inside the earth. Today, many anthropologists believe the first North Americans came from Asia across the Bering Land Bridge that connected Alaska to Russia during the last ice age. In one sense, how these people came to Alaska doesn't matter, nor does where they came from. Their stories, memories, and traditions all grew out of the Alaskan landscape.

This creation story was told to naturalist Edward W. Nelson during his travels in Alaska in the late nineteenth century.

With diverse cultures and a rich traditional heritage, Native Alaskans are tied to the land in every aspect of life.

Photo © Alaska Division of Tourism. Used by permission.

In the beginning there was water over all the earth, and it was very cold; the water was covered with ice, and there were no people. Then the ice ground together, making long ridges and hummocks. At this time came a man from the far side of the great water and stopped on the ice hills near where Pikmiktalik now is, taking for his wife a she-wolf. By and by he had many children, which were always born in pairs—a boy and a girl. Each pair spoke a tongue of their own, different from that of their parents and different from any spoken by their brothers and sisters.

As soon as they were large enough each pair was sent out in a different direction from the others, and thus the family spread far and near from the ice hills, which now became

Inupiat &
St. Lawrence Island
Yup'ik

Athabascan

Yup'ik & Cup'ik

Eyak, Tlingit,
Haida, &
Tsimshian

Aleut (Unangax^)

Native Alaskans are diverse, with many cultural and geographic groups; about twenty languages are spoken by the various groups.

snow-covered mountains. As the snow melted it ran down the hill-sides, scooping out ravines and river beds, and so making the earth with its streams.

The twins peopled the earth with their children, and as each pair with their children spoke a language different from the others, the various tongues found on the earth were established and continue until this day.

(Edward W. Nelson, *The Eskimo About Bering Strait* [Washington, DC: Smithsonian Institution, 1899; reprinted 1983], 482)

Native Alaskans are diverse. Divided by geography and language, there are three main groups with many subgroups and dialects in each region.

Eskimos

Most knitters in the Oomingmak Co-op are Eskimos from the western coast of Alaska. The people toward the south, living in the Yukon-Kuskokwim Delta area, are known as Yup'ik. (The Siberian Yup'ik of St. Lawrence Island and the Cup'ik of Nunivak Island are closely related to mainland Yup'ik, but speak distinct dialects.) The Inupiat, living in the northern part of the state, are closely related to the Inuit of Canada and Greenland. Although the Yup'ik and Inupiat have many similarities, the two groups speak separate languages, about as different from each other as English is from German.

Aleuts

Several Aleutian knitters belonged to the co-op in the past, but few are actively involved today. This culture, found on the Aleutian archipelago at the southwestern tip of Alaska, was changed drastically by the presence of Russian traders, whose influences can still be seen in the area. Boats and sea travel have always been central to the Aleutian way of life, and the people traveled widely in small qayaqs and larger angyaqs to hunt, fish, and trade with other peoples in Alaska.

Indians

The Native Alaskans living in the southeastern parts of the state include the Eyak, Tlingit, Haida, and Tsimshian Indians. These groups, known as the Northwest Coast Peoples, have much in common with Native Americans living on the Pacific coast in Canada and as far south as Oregon. The Athabascan Indians inhabit the interior of the state. With eleven languages and dialects, the Indians are the most diverse group of Alaskan Natives.

Oomingmak Musk Ox Producers' Co-op provides an income source for the knitters while they preserve their cultural heritage and take pride in the quality of their fine needlework.

Needlework: Women's art

Knitting was not introduced to Alaska until European missionaries arrived in the eighteenth century, but Inupiat women have long been renowned for their skill with the needle.

According to tradition, these women gained their abilities in a magical and fascinating way.

Very long ago there were many men living in the northland, but there was no woman living among them. Far away in the southland a single woman was known to live. At last one of the young men in the north started and traveled to the south until he came to the woman's house, where he stopped and in a short time he became her husband. One day he sat in the house thinking of his home and said, 'Ah, I have a wife, while the son of the headman in the north has none.' And he was much pleased in thinking of his good fortune.

Meanwhile the headman's son also had set out to journey toward the south, and while the husband was talking to himself the son stood in the entrance passage to the house listening to him. He waited there in the passage until the people inside were asleep. Then he crept into the house and, seizing the woman by the shoulder, began dragging her away.

Just as he reached the doorway he was overtaken by the husband, who caught the woman by her feet. Then followed a struggle, which ended by pulling the woman in two, the thief carrying the upper half of the body away to his home in the northland, while the husband was left with the lower half of his wife. Each man set to work to replace the missing parts from carved wood. After these were fitted on they became endowed with life, and so two women were made from the halves of one.

The woman in the south, however, was a poor needlewoman, owing to the clumsiness of her wooden fingers, but was a fine dancer. The woman in

Winter parkas were made from fur, warm-weather parkas from feathers, and waterproof gear from fishskin or seal gut. This is Mrs. Sophia Nun, wearing a fur parka.

Photo courtesy of Archives, Alaska and Polar Regions Collections, Rasmuson Library, University of Alaska Fairbanks. Used by permission.

Yup'ik seamstresses stored their tools in sewing kits called housewives. Made from seal- and fishskins, these beautiful cases exhibit many of the same designs and shapes used in clothing.

the north was very expert in needlework, but her wooden legs made her a very poor dancer. Each of these women gave to her daughters these characteristics, so that to the present time the same difference is noted between the women of the north and those of the south, thus showing that the tale is true."

(Edward W. Nelson, *The Eskimo About Bering Strait* [Washington, DC: Smithsonian Institution, 1899; reprinted 1983], 479)

In reality, Eskimo women throughout Alaska excelled in both skin sewing and needlework. Inupiat women stitched exquisite fur and skin parkas, frocks, boots, gloves, and mittens to keep their families warm during the long arctic winters. Decorated with detailed embroidery and intricate patchwork designs sewn from tiny pieces of fur, Inupiat garments were both stylish and functional. In southern Alaska, Yup'ik women were honored for their talent as nimble dancers, but, contrary to legend, they made garments that were as meticulously stitched as, if less ornately decorated than, those of their northern neighbors.

Beginning in the late 1800s, Eskimo artists developed new types of arts and crafts, such as making baleen baskets and ivory cribbage boards, for the tourist trade. The qiviut lace scarves of Oomingmak Musk Ox Producers' Co-operative belong to this tradition. Although these tourist products are often not respected as "authentic" art, they are beautiful examples of artwork created to fill a need in a culture adapting to change.

Inupiat women stored sealskin thimbles and ivory needles in elaborately carved needle cases.

Both objects are from the University of Alaska Museum of the North Collection. Above: Kakivik (sewing bag) and rolled-up sewing bag, catalog number ACC595 with M5876. Right: Bone needle case from Pelly Bay, Nunavut, Canada, catalog number UA68-52-6. Used by permission. Photos by Angela Linn.

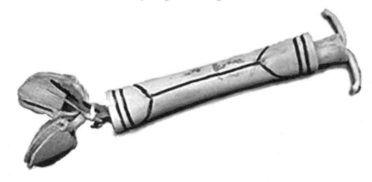

House and home

The Yup'ik and Inupiat Eskimos have a rich culture that has been adapting to change for hundreds of years. Unlike the Eskimos in northern Canada and Greenland, the Yup'ik and Inupiat who live near the Bering Sea never lived in ice igloos but built underground houses covered with sod. Today, these traditional sod houses have been replaced by modern homes.

This story, told by Lucy Nuqarrluk Daniels, is about one family's experience with change and tradition in the twentieth century.

The entrance to a traditional subterranean home was a long tunnel dug into the ground below the level of the house. The tunnel trapped cold air and, with the help of body heat and seal-oil lamps, kept the inside warm and snug during the coldest months of the year.

Photo courtesy of Alaska State Library, Historical Collections, Juneau. Used by permission. Taken at Mekoryuk, Nunivak Island.

I was born in the fall of 1946 in a small Yup'ik Eskimo village in southeast Alaska. I grew up in a time that now seems like ancient Alaska. In the left back corner of our one-room frame house sat a double-sized bed, commercially made, where Mom, Dad and my little sister, and I slept. My spot was right next to the wall by my sister, who slept next to Mom, who slept next to Dad.

Grandma, Dad's mother, slept in a twin bed—a network of wires on a metal frame—in the right back corner. Grandpa, Mom's father, slept in a wooden twin-sized bed in the right front corner. The wood stove took up the remaining corner. . . .

Every spring, Grandpa dug flowing ditches to drain mud puddles. I floated many a wood chip down those ditches. . . .

Springtime meant melting snow, Grandpa's drainage ditches, and spring camp. Every April, Mom and Dad pulled my brother and me out of school and took the family to spring camp. Nestled among our belongings in the sled, we took a leisurely dog-team ride to camp.

The traditional sod house had one seal-gut window in the roof to let in light and, when opened, to release smoke.

Photo courtesy of Archives, Alaska and Polar Regions Collections, Rasmuson Library, University of Alaska Fairbanks. Used by permission. Abandoned sod house.

From our camp we heard the sounds of waterfowl all around us. I especially remember the eerie crying of the loon. Mom and Grandma cut and dried pike and skinned countless muskrat. I helped string the slimy, slithery blackfish onto willow branches to prepare for drying.

Grandma took me along when she went to check the fish net or went egg hunting. I can still hear the swish, swish, swish of the paddle as Grandma guided the canoe over placid waters.

Looking for eggs at an egg-hunting site, I trudged behind Grandma over the spongy tundra. When a mother bird fluttered away ahead of us, we found its eggs right away. When it circled around and around above us, Grandma instructed me to lie down on the ground beside her. When the bird had landed, we walked to where it lay roosting. When we found the nest, Grandma put the eggs into a moss-lined pail, removed the lining of the nest, spit on it, and placed it beside the nest. I still don't know why.

At camp, Grandpa's homemade bow and arrows kept me entertained. Patiently, Grandpa whittled a replacement for each lost arrow. In wintertime, he made me a wooden or moose-horn "storyknife." In the snow that drifted into the porch, my friend and I told each other stories. We flattened and smoothed over a place on the snow (or mud in summertime) with the storyknife to roughly the size of an 8" x 11" sheet of paper. We drew symbols of the various parts of the story as we talked.

Today's housing projects have made our one-room house a part of a pleasant childhood memory. A network of boardwalks in my home village has rendered Grandpa's drainage ditches quite unnecessary. Commercial chicken eggs, tasteless by comparison, have replaced wild bird eggs. . . . Spring camps are a thing of the past. BB guns have antiquated Grandpa's bows and arrows. TV, the VCR, and "Super Mario" have become more interesting than "storyknifing."

(Lucy Nuqarrluk Daniels, "Writer Grows Up Eskimo in 'Ancient' Alaska," in *Authentic Alaska,* Susan B. Andrews and John Creed [Lincoln, NE: Bison Books, 1998], 23–25)

Before modern housing was introduced to rural Alaska, communities used driftwood (in the Yukon-Kuskokwim Delta) and whale ribs (north of the Bering Strait) covered with sod to build large *qassiq,* or community gathering places, and smaller *enu,* or family homes.

Men and older boys spent their days in the qassiq, commonly called a men's house. At night, married men usually slept in their family homes, but single men and orphans stayed in the men's house. The qassiq also served as a community center for annual festivals and for housing visitors from other villages.

Women, girls, and small boys lived in small family homes. The family did everything from cooking and preparing meals to tanning skins and giving birth in these small dwellings. It was here, also, that mothers and grandmothers taught young girls.

With their cultural diversity, rich environment, and subarctic climate, the people of coastal Alaska were never like the stereotypical Eskimos that so many of us learned about. Textbooks depicting snowbound Eskimos with rosy cheeks rubbing noses to kiss and eating only raw meat are terribly out of date and demeaning. This picture is not at all representative of the lifestyle of the Yup'ik and Inupiat peoples of Alaska.

Even today, Native Alaskan children reading approved textbooks often fail to recognize themselves in the sections about Eskimos. They are confused and offended when their culture is not depicted accurately, when their traditions are not part of the standard curriculum, and when their people are not honored as the first Alaskans.

Sod houses were used in some parts of Alaska as late as the 1970s.

Photo courtesy of Archives and Manuscripts Department, Consortium Library, University of Alaska Anchorage. Used by permission. Mekoryuk, Nunivak Island, June 1948.

Subsistence

Western Alaska is a lush, abundant environment rich with wild plants, year-round supplies of fish, and easily accessible land and marine mammals that serve as food sources. Although winters are cold and dark, summers are warm and bright, bringing forth an amazing array of wild berries, greens, and grasses.

This story by Julia Jones Anausuk Stalker celebrates traditional, local foods.

I am originally from Selawik, which is where I grew up in the 1960s. I recall the days in Selawik when we had only Native food to eat. It is called *niqipiaq*, meaning food prepared off the land. In those days store-bought foods were so scarce, we ate niqipiaq almost every day. Today, we still enjoy those foods and sharing the delicious meals and the company of others and indulging in our favorite foods that are set on the table.

Niqipiaq is served for many occasions including family gatherings such as birthdays, holidays, or a welcoming party for visiting family. At such events the table will be filled with a variety of niqipiaq. You have a choice of which food you want to eat, such as dried caribou meat and dried fish: white, pike, or salmon. Frozen white fish, or trout (*quaq*), is laid on the table to thaw just enough to easily cut. Seal oil is also placed on the table.

Vegetables that are rendered in seal oil spice up one's plate. These vegetables include a certain kind of leaves called sura and wild celery, which is rare today. Berries for dessert also are placed on the table, which is the best part of the meal for a satisfied stomach. Salmonberries (*aqpiks*), blackberries, and blueberries are mixed in a bowl and usually served plain or as Eskimo ice cream.

Besides taking pleasure in the eating, we are taught to hunt the right kind of animal or pick the right plants to prepare these foods at the right time. A book about this called *Plants That We Eat*, written by Anore Jones, was dedicated to the "Old-time Eskimo people, Utuqqanaat Iñupiat" and to "The young Eskimo people, Nutaat Iñupiat." It shows

Reindeer meat dries on wooden racks in the same fashion as fish.

Photo courtesy of Archives, Alaska and Polar Regions Collections, Rasmuson Library, University of Alaska Fairbanks. Used by permission.

where and what to pick in the summer. The dedication adds a message to the Iñupiat: "That they may learn and use it, blending the best with other culture . . . and that they may pass it on."

Gathering and storing of food have changed greatly. In the days of my late grandfather, life was hard. To hunt, the Iñupiat went on foot, by *qayaq* (canoe), or with dog teams. They did not have snow-machines to rely on, nor did they have freezers to save their food. According to Elmer Imgusriq Ballot, an Elder who told a story in the lore of the Iñupiat entitled "Ways That Are No More," "We did not enjoy any frozen food during the summer as people do now."

Native food also fills a hunter's grub box. My dad was a great hunter as I recall. He knew when and where to go for all the different food. For survival, he took along a grub box full of niqipiaq in case he got trapped in bad weather. My mom in the same manner went out to pick greens and fruit off the land.

The foods we eat also connect us with the experience of going out in the country. Our energy comes from the land we live on. Our health and happiness are restored by our daily diet. Niqipiaq has all the vitamins and minerals that our bodies require. A similar philosophy is expressed by people of another culture: authors Michio and Aveline Kushi who wrote *Macrobiotic Dietary Recommendations*, stating that "food is our source of being" and that "to eat is to take in the whole environment." We all have such a way to connect our lives to the earth.

Today, we are encouraged to continue this essential part of our Iñupiaq heritage. For our children and their children, we know how important it is to feed from our land while we still can. Our foods define who we are, connect us to the land and keep our culture alive.

(Julia Jones Anausuk Stalker, "Native Food Nourishes the Body and More," in *Authentic Alaska*, Susan B. Andrews and John Creed [Lincoln, NE: Bison Books, 1998], 30–31)

Using sinew nets and wooden traps, men set out to catch enough salmon to last through the coming winter.

Photo courtesy of Archives, Alaska State Library, Historical Collections, Juneau. Used by permission. Best trap maker in the village, Kalskag, Alaska, February 1940.

Changing economy

For the Eskimos of Alaska, contact with Outsiders came much later than it did for Native Americans in the lower forty-eight states, and with somewhat less disastrous consequences. That's not to say that contact between cultures was without conflict or devastation. Although the Yup'ik and Inupiat people were not driven off their traditional lands and forced onto distant reservations, they still faced disease, prejudice, and unprecedented change.

This short selection of prose and poetry by Geri Reich, who lives and works at the Red Dog Mine above the Arctic Circle for six months out of the year, shows how difficult it is for women in the area to work at the available jobs, often many miles away from their homes and families. Still, where these jobs are available, many women will take the higher pay instead of the few dollars that can be made knitting.

Sometimes as I fly out of Kotzebue to go back to work at the Red Dog Mine, I remember the first time I took this route a few years ago in July 1988, my first day on the job.

Although Red Dog's location ninety miles above the Arctic Circle brings frigid temperatures most of the year, on this brilliant summer's day, the perpetual sun's heat stifled the crowded cabin in Baker Aviation's Cessna 402 as we left Kotzebue's airport runway.

Snowmobiles and four-wheelers have largely replaced dog teams for winter transportation in rural Alaska.

Photo © Barry Whitehill, Alaska Division of Tourism. Used by permission.

Small fishing boats bobbed in the waves below as we flew north over Kotzebue Sound. Normally, I would have been on one of those boats, commercial fishing.

Instead, I was leaving Kotzebue, the small, dusty, remote town in Northwest Alaska where I was born, where I grew up. I had agreed to live and work—at least for the next six months—in an even more remote place. Ambivalence crowded my mind. "What was I doing? Is all this worth my time?"

I was again leaving my two children, then eight-year-old A.J. and twelve-year-old Jennifer, for a long time. I had just completed five months of electrical training at the Alaska Vocational Technical center in Seward, hundreds of miles from Kotzebue. I ached to be a normal mother and just stay home, baking cookies for my kids. . . .

Sadness envelopes me today
Like the dark, wet blanket of fog
That falls over Seward
Every child I see
Reminds me of you
I long for the sunshine of home
Where it allows me always to watch over you
Soon, when the darkness lifts
We'll be together again
As we should be
I miss you
My babies.

These feelings still haunt me to this day as I travel back and forth . . . for my job.

(Geri Reich, "Iñupiat Woman Balances Work, Family Reponsibilities," in *Authentic Alaska*, Susan B. Andrews and John Creed [Lincoln, NE: Bison Books, 1998], 145–146, 150)

"I long for the sunshine of home

Where it allows me always to watch over you. . . ."

Geri Reich

Modern culture

Like many in the United States, today's Alaskan Eskimos embrace new technology, comforts, and conveniences while looking back with nostalgia on a pristine past. But unlike many immigrants who struggle to assimilate into mainstream American culture, Native Alaskans strive to keep their traditions alive.

In this narrative, Verné Seum examines the differences between her mother's and her grandfather's generations.

My mother and grandfather are people whom I love very much. Both are full-blooded Iñupiaq Eskimos. Nevertheless, they exhibit definite contrasts, reflecting two different eras.

My grandfather, a man of sixty-two years, is characterized by white hair and a stoic face. He has stern, piercing eyes that seem to read the thoughts of the souls of those with whom he speaks. He conserves his smiles for moments of true satisfaction, in which he celebrates quietly. His five-foot, ten-inch, 210-pound frame commands the utmost respect from those around him. He believes questions are unnecessary and that learning through observing accomplishes understanding. At this point in his life, my grandfather kicks back and enjoys his retirement.

My mother, at forty-one, has deep black hair that complements her compassionate face. Her gentle, loving smile is mirrored by the luster of her glimmering black eyes. She is an outgoing, witty woman who is proud of her heritage. She has a petite build of five feet, two inches, and weighs 104 pounds. Unlike my grandfather, my mother's views are contemporary. She believes that in order to avoid confusion, verbal communication is necessary. Far from retirement, my mother loves working.

My grandfather, after raising children for forty-one years, now leaves that chore behind him. He still makes his opinions on raising children known: His conservative ideas on education lead him to believe that children should learn at home with their families. In this case, chores take first priority over extracurricular activities.

With the availability of television, video games, wireless Internet, and satellite phones, the young people in Yup'ik and Inupiat villages live in a world of both traditional and modern expectations.

Photo © Alaska Division of Tourism. Used by permission.

Far different, my mother, in raising five children, encourages obtaining formal education to supplement life's experiences. Her goal is that we continue our education after high school. To her, homework always comes first.

The conflicting influences these two individuals bestow upon my life often cause problems. My mother, liberated and independent, has one son in his freshman year of college, a daughter in her last year of high school and enrolled in college courses, and a daughter in seventh grade moving ahead scholastically and determined to go to college. My mother always pushes us to do our best in school.

In complete contrast to my mother's modern views, my grandfather believes that women have their duties and should be submissive. Influenced by my grandfather, my brother has learned some of the traditional ways of hunting and fishing. In my grandfather's household, my sister and I maintain the house and cook for our uncles. We also have learned that we have to budget our time effectively, because he feels we spend too much time at school and school activities.

Here are two people that I love dearly, but what a contrast!

My grandfather lives in a time past, a time when tradition was the only way to survive, when education could only be taught through informal means, and a time when women and men had definite roles that insured the survival of the people. To him, this life is secure. He fails to understand why our generation can't live the life he has led.

My mother, however, remembers the past, lives for today, and prepares for tomorrow. She doesn't ignore tradition but insists that we are able to adjust to new conditions. To her, the world is modern, where acceleration and advancement are the means of survival. She believes the way to advance is to increase one's education in the formal classroom. She lives the life of an independent woman.

To her, to be educated is to be secure.

(Verné Seum, "New Paths, Old Ways," in *Authentic Alaska*, Susan B. Andrews and John Creed [Lincoln, NE: Bison Books, 1998], 142–143)

The Yup'ik and Inupiat peoples may not have ever been the peaceful and "noble savages" that explorers from other parts of the world imagined, but even today they continue to respect the land and consider the effects of their decisions, not only on their own lives but on the lives of their descendants for seven generations.

Spring in Unalakleet.

Chapter 3

Villages and knitters

Learning about the history and cultures of Alaska from books and museums was interesting, but to truly understand the members of the Oomingmak Co-op, I wanted to visit the knitters where they live. The co-op works with knitters in small villages scattered across Alaska. I would have liked to visit all of the villages, but because travel in rural Alaska is expensive I was only able to visit Unalakleet, a village on Norton Sound.

I was nervous about the visit, afraid that the experience would be completely foreign to me. After meeting Marie, Eliza, and Joyce at the Oomingmak shop, I was a bit less anxious. Even so, I knew the pace would be slower and the attitude more relaxed than anything I'd experienced before.

As soon as our tiny plane landed at the Unalakleet airport, I realized that my nervous anticipation had been unnecessary. I was both relieved and disappointed to find that Unalakleet was not so much an "Eskimo village" as a typical American rural town. I don't know what I expected, but what I found was a small community much like any other. It reminded me of Encampment, Wyoming, a few hours' drive from my home in Colorado. A graffiti-splattered trailer proclaimed "Mötley Crüe Rules!," but around the corner, wolverine skins hanging to dry suggested that I was actually far from home. When I looked more closely, I saw signs of the Eskimo way of life all over town: teams of huskies slept on the tops of homemade doghouses in many yards; log-framed fish-drying houses were scattered around town and along the beach; and fishing boats in dry dock for the winter were everywhere.

The town is amazingly tiny. When we arrived, I called Mike, the owner of Brown's Lodge, to pick us up at the airport, although we later learned we could have walked from the airfield on the north end of town to the lodge at the south end in fifteen minutes. With no paved roads, no street signs, no signs on stores, a small post office, a general store, and only two Alaska state troopers, Unalakleet is more rural than any place I have visited before. Even so, most people have trucks, snowmobiles, and four-wheelers. In the 50-degree F (10-degree C) weather, the kids were out with spring fever, cruising all around town. Inside the lodge with the window open, it sounded like I was on Mission Bay in San Diego, surrounded by a sea of jet skis.

Everyone I met in Unalakleet spoke English. On my trip to the village, I heard only one family speaking Yup'ik and that was at the airport in Anchorage. Even the children playing in the public library spoke English; perhaps they speak Yup'ik or Inupiat at home with their parents.

While in Unalakleet, I met Fran Degnan, who is a knitter and an author. Her book, *Under the Arctic Sun*, tells the story of her parents, Frank and Ada Degnan, and their lives in rural Alaska. As I read Fran's book, I realized that Unalakleet is every bit as cosmopolitan as New York City. Fran's family tree includes Yup'ik, Inupiat, Swedish, German, French Canadian, Irish, and Russian ancestors. The Unalakleet phone books list as many European surnames as Yup'ik and Inupiat. Although the population of most Alaskan villages is over 90 percent Native, marriages between local residents and visitors have been common since the first contact with Outsiders, and parents often give their children both Eskimo

Boats are everywhere. In winter, every yard boasts at least one boat in dry dock. In summer, travel over the spongy ground is almost impossible and boats become the "cars" of the tundra. They are in constant use for commercial fishing, subsistence activities, and transportation.

Dominic Cotignola

Dominic Cotignola

Fran Degnan, an author who writes for the Musk Ox Farm's newsletter, has participated in the Oomingmak Co-op as a knitter for almost twenty years.

and Christian names. It seems that while nineteenth- and twentieth-century urban centers in Alaska were filled with prejudice, in the rural areas, many people—of whatever origins—were bound together by the experience of living off the land. The place is definitely a melting pot!

Most of the co-op knitters live in villages like Unalakleet near the Bering Sea and in Alaska's river deltas. As you approach from the air, these small towns, most with between 100 and 700 inhabitants, look like they have been constructued from Monopoly game pieces. Only Bethel, the commercial hub of the Yukon-Kuskokwim Delta—with almost 6,000 people, a hospital, a fire station, and pizza delivery—is almost suburban.

In summer, each solitary community rises out of an expanse of green and blue, tundra and sea surrounding small centers of human population. In winter, piles of snow tower overhead, casting skyscraper shadows over a maze of freshly plowed roads that are dirt underneath. Surrounded on all sides by snow and ice, white extending in all directions, the villages seem to float in space. Only piles of driftwood lining the shore reveal where the frozen sea ends and the land begins.

Nothing from urban areas reaches these remote locations by wire or pipeline. Satellite phones connect family members at home to their relatives in urban centers. Electricity is produced locally using diesel or wind generators. Plumbing systems are also local. Some villages pipe or truck water to each home, and city sewers provide safe and clean systems for disposing of waste. In smaller villages with no indoor plumbing, people haul water to their homes from public spigots and empty their "honeybuckets" at community "sewage lagoons."

Without roads to connect these outposts scattered along Alaska's coasts and river deltas, I wondered where people could go in the trucks I saw on the dirt roads in town. To a visitor more accustomed to urban living, isolation and loneliness seem to lurk behind every snowdrift. A simple visit to friends or loved ones requires a long trip by snow-go (snowmobile), dog sled, or bush plane. General stores are sparsely stocked with merchandise flown in from Anchorage or Fairbanks, and, because of the

Dominic Cotignola

The villages along the Bering Sea continue to evolve, merging traditional and modern cultures.

transportation, all the goods were much more expensive than I expected. These remote islands of humanity are invisible on satellite maps; no streetlights reveal their location in the darkness; no light pollution blocks out the brightness of the Milky Way. To Wal-Mart and NASA, rural Alaska does not exist.

And yet life and creativity abound in these remote places. As traditional values collide with modernity, the knitters of Oomingmak see Alaska changing before their eyes. Because I could visit only one village during my trip, I extended my understanding by writing to knitters around the state and asking them about their lives and knitting.

Katie Baker Tootkaylook learned to knit in a workshop when the co-op was first established in the 1960s. "Remembering those first years," she said in her letter, "it was hard. But as days went on, I learned to knit quite well and I taught others how to knit." Today Katie doesn't participate in subsistence activities. But she grew up on Nunivak Island in a sod house adjacent to her village's *qassiq* (men's house) before commercial products were available on the island. "There was no modern food," she recalls. "I grew up on Native food."

Grace Harrod's father wanted his daughter to get a good education and sent her to high school in Sitka. After graduating, she lived in Anchorage until she moved to Kodiak, where she lives today with her husband. She says, "I am Cup'ik, but I'd never seen an igloo in my whole childhood, until Mr. Gibson, the teacher from Seattle, Washington, showed us how to make one in grade school."

Katherine Charles, who grew up in Newtok, knits to ward off boredom. "Whenever I have nothing to do," she says, "I just sit down and start knitting. My knitting is being bought by people from all over the place and that makes me want to knit more. When I see someone wearing a musk ox knitted nachaq, scarf, or stole, I often wonder, 'Did I knit that?'" For the Charles family, berry picking and fishing are family activities. Katherine says, "My kids love to travel by boat because before they turn a year old, we start taking them camping."

Tilly Dull, who learned to knit from her mother when she was a small girl, remembers, " . . . making things that I could wear—like slippers and hats. I made many mistakes but was determined to do it correctly." Today Tilly is a full-time teacher who likes to knit nachaqs whenever she can, "especially when traveling."

The following pages provide a tour of many of the villages where the knitters of Oomingmak Musk Ox Producers' Co-operative live, work, and raise their families.

Above: To highlight its unique heritage and culture, each original village of the Oomingmak Musk Ox Producers' Co-operative has a signature knitting pattern adapted from a design found in traditional Eskimo art. This is the Star Cap from the traditional line, worn with a scarf.

Right: New communities joining the co-op knit the signature lace patterns of nearby villages or the Tundra and Snow color-work patterns that have recently been introduced. These are Herder's Caps, from the Tundra and Snow line.

Photos by Chris Arend, courtesy of Chris Arend and Oomingmak Musk Ox Producers' Co-operative.

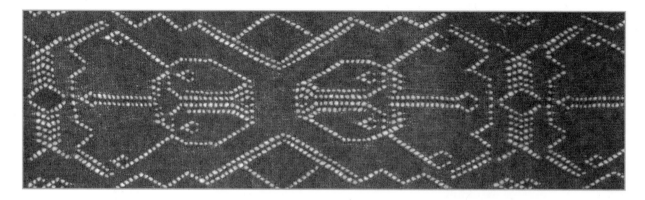

Unalakleet

The Wolverine Mask pattern knitted in Unalakleet was adapted from a mask used in traditional dance festivals. This is a rare pattern.

Knitted in lightweight yarn. Photo by Bill Bacon, courtesy of Bill Bacon and Oomingmak Musk Ox Producers' Co-operative.

Unalakleet, which means "south side," was historically the southern-most village in Inupiat territory. Unalakleet is said to have been the first settlement in North America. Lying on the border between Yup'ik and Inupiat lands, the village was an important trading hub. Archaeologists date the first settlement here, near what is now the airport, to 200 or 300 BCE. About 500 years ago, after the ancient village was abandoned, a second village was established on the south side of the Unalakleet River. The Russian American Company built a trading post across the river from the village in the early 1830s. When a smallpox epidemic wiped out almost the entire community in 1838 and 1839, the thirteen survivors moved to the north side of the river and established the community that is still thriving.

Early Christian missionaries prohibited the making of traditional masks worn during dances and festivals. Today the Yup'ik and Inupiat people once again make masks and celebrate their heritage with traditional dances.

These are the Savoonga Eskimo Dancers performing at the Alaska Native Heritage Center in Anchorage.

Photo © Loren Taft / Accent Alaska. com. Used by permission.

Located on Norton Sound, Unalakleet has been home to Inupiat Eskimos for almost 2,000 years.

Today, Unalakleet is also a popular recreation area. The upper portion of the Unalakleet River has been designated as a National Wild and Scenic River, and an upscale fishing lodge offers tours and fishing trips during the summer season. Each year, the Iditarod Trail Sled Dog Race passes through Unalakleet and turns north along the coast toward its final destination in Nome.

Unalakleet joined the Oomingmak Co-op in 1976. Since then, thirty-two knitters have made scarves and nachaqs with the Wolverine Mask pattern. Unalakleet was also home to the Musk Ox Farm from 1975 to 1984.

Unalakleet	
(yoo'-nuh-luh-kleet)	
Population	710
Location	Norton Sound 148 miles (238 km) southeast of Nome 395 miles (636 km) northwest of Anchorage
Area (land)	2.9 square miles (7.5 sq km)
Area (water)	2.3 square miles (6 sq km)
Elevation	8–12 feet (2.4–3.7 m)
Climate	Subarctic
Precipitation	14 inches (35.6 cm) annual average
Snowfall	41 inches (104.1 cm) annual average

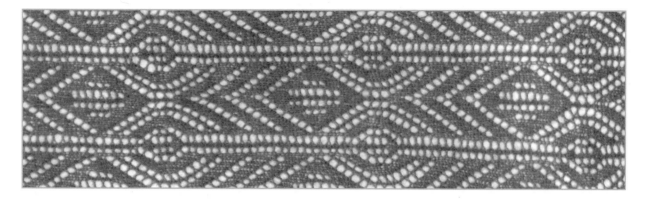

Mekoryuk

The Harpoon pattern, adapted from a carving on a 1,200-year-old ivory harpoon head found on Nunivak Island, was originally knitted as a single pattern on a solid stockinette-stitch background. Later, the design was modified to include several interlaced harpoon patterns for a lacier effect. The pattern is used for scarves, stoles, and nachaqs.

Knitted in lightweight yarn. Photo by Bill Bacon, courtesy of Bill Bacon and Oomingmak Musk Ox Producers' Co-operative.

The people of Mekoryuk, the only village on Nunivak Island, are Cup'ik Eskimos. Although closely related to the Yup'ik people, they have a distinct dialect and a unique culture, the result of inhabiting an island for about 2,000 years. In 1821 explorers from the Russian American Company visited Nunivak Island and found 400 people living in sixteen separate villages. What is now Mekoryuk was then a summer camp called Koot. In 1900 an epidemic wiped out the entire population of the island, except for four families.

Hans Himmelheber, a German ethnologist, visited Nunivak Island in 1936 and again in 1985. On his first visit, the people lived in underground sod igloos, and the men gathered in the qassiq. Upon his return almost fifty years later, not a single subterranean dwelling remained. Instead he noticed a traffic sign giving direction to "the two motorcars on the island."

Larger than Long Island, New York, Nunivak Island is the seventh largest island in the United States. Now part of the Yukon Delta National Wildlife Refuge, it is home to herds of reindeer and musk oxen. In 1934, after the musk ox had been extinct in Alaska for about fifty years, thirty-four animals were transplanted from Greenland to Nunivak Island in an attempt to reintroduce the species. This is also where the first animals for the Musk Ox Farm were captured. Today there are more than 500 animals on the island.

Mekoryuk was the first village to join the Oomingmak Co-op. Since that time, 108 knitters have worked Mekoryuk's signature pattern, the Harpoon.

Alaska

Mekoryuk

In 1968 Ann Lillian Schell, textile expert for the co-op, visited Nunivak Island and taught the first group of knitters how to work with qiviut yarn and read the unusual charted patterns.

Early workshop. Photo courtesy of Oomingmak Musk Ox Producers' Co-operative.

Mekoryuk, on Nunivak Island, is home to the Cup'ik people and was the first village to join Oomingmak Musk Ox Producers' Co-operative.

Mekoryuk	
(ma-kor'-ee-yuck)	
Population	192
Location	Nunivak Island 149 miles (240 km) west of Bethel 553 miles (890 km) west of Anchorage
Area (land)	7.4 square miles (19.2 sq km)
Area (water)	0.1 square mile (.26 sq km)
Elevation	40 feet (12 m)
Climate	Cool, rainy summers with frequent fog and storms
Precipitation	15 inches (38.1 cm) annual average
Snowfall	57 inches (144.8 cm) annual average

Bethel and Quinhagak

Knitters in Bethel and Quinhagak work the Butterfly design, inspired by the trim on parkas and kuspuks. This pattern is used on scarves and nachaqs.

Photo by Bill Bacon, courtesy of Bill Bacon and Oomingmak Musk Ox Producers' Co-operative.

In 1885 Bethel was founded by Moravian missionaries across the river from a Yup'ik village called Mamterillermiut or Mumtrekhlogamute. The original name means "smokehouse people," referring to a nearby place to smoke fish. The missionaries named their community Bethel, after the biblical city. A local shaman warned the missionaries that the river would "rise and eat the ground beneath their houses," but the missionaries didn't listen. The shaman was apparently right; Bethel moved to its current location because of erosion.

An excellent fishing location and a trading center for the region, Bethel has become the largest city in the Yukon-Kuskokwim Delta. It is home to many government agencies, a regional hospital and family health clinic, the Kuskokwim Campus of the University of Alaska Fairbanks, and the Yupiit Piciryarait Cultural Center and Museum. Located inside the Yukon Delta National Wildlife Refuge, Bethel is also an outstanding home base for bird-watching and wildlife-viewing excursions.

Problems with pollution, overfishing, and climate change have affected Bethel. Since 1997 the community has suffered from unusually low fish harvests. With fishing as a primary source of food and income in the area, this is a crisis.

Kuspuks, the traditional summer parkas worn by Yup'ik and Inupiat women, are now often made from brightly colored cotton.

Photo © Alaska Division of Tourism. Used by permission.

Located near the Bering Sea, Bethel and Quinhagak are examples of the diversity of rural Alaska.

Bethel is ten times larger than Quinhagak. It is home to many government agencies and regional businesses, while Quinhagak, its neighbor to the south, focuses on Yup'ik subsistence activities and traditional crafts, such as basket weaving and skin sewing.

Alaska

Bethel & Quinhagak

Quinhagak, or Kwinhagak, 71 miles (114 km) from Bethel, was the first Alaskan village to have continuous contact with Outsiders. The original village, established about 1,000 years ago, was named Kuinerraq, meaning "new river channel." In the late nineteenth century, many non-Natives lived in Quinhagak, a key port for transporting goods to trading posts along the Kuskokwim River. Today, the village population is almost entirely Yup'ik.

Bethel joined the Oomingmak Co-op in 1971 and Quinhagak joined in 1981. The 59 knitters who have participated from both villages knit the Butterfly motif.

	Bethel	Quinhagak
	(beth'-ul)	(quinn'-uh-hawk)
Population	5,960	642
Location	400 miles (644 km) west of Anchorage	71 miles (114 km) southwest of Bethel
Area (land)	43.8 square miles (113.4 sq km)	4.7 square miles (12.2 sq km)
Area (water)	5.1 square miles (13.2 sq km)	0.6 square mile (1.6 sq km)
Elevation	10 feet (3 m)	10 feet (3 m)
Climate	Maritime (influenced by airflow from the ocean	Maritime (influenced by airflow from the ocean)
Precipitation	16 inches (40.6 cm) annual average	22 inches (55.9 cm) annual average
Snowfall	50 inches (127 cm) annual average	43 inches (109.2 cm) annual average

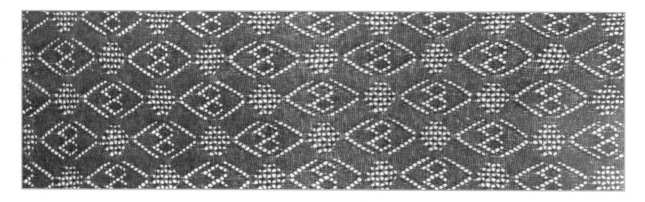

Nelson Island

The Nelson Island Diamond pattern is knitted by co-op members from several small villages on and near Nelson Island. Like Bethel's signature pattern, this design was adapted from the trim on parkas and kuspuks. It is used on scarves, stoles, and nachaqs.

Knitted in lightweight yarn. Photo by Bill Bacon, courtesy of Bill Bacon and Oomingmak Musk Ox Producers' Co-operative.

About half the size of Nunivak Island, Nelson Island is home to several Yup'ik villages and a herd of wild musk oxen. The people of the area are known as Qaluyaarmiut or "dip net people." They have lived on the island for about 2,000 years and had little contact with Outsiders before the 1920s. The island was named for Edward Nelson, a naturalist from the Smithsonian Institution who visited the area in 1878.

Four villages on the island have knitters in the Oomingmak Co-op. Knitters from all of these villages knit the Nelson Island Diamond pattern, adapted from designs found on parka and kuspuk trims. In 1971 Nightmute was the first village in the area to join the co-op; Tununak and Toksook Bay followed in 1976; and Newtok

In winter, the Alaska Department of Fish and Game issues a limited number of hunting permits when the population of the musk ox herd on Nelson Island exceeds 250.

Photo © Brent Huffman. www.ultimateungulate.com. Used by permission.

Alaska

Nelson Island

Newtok, Nightmute, Toksook Bay, and Tununak are located near the coast on Kangirlvar Bay. The Yup'ik name for the island is Qaluyaaq.

joined in 1982. During the past thirty years, 126 knitters have made scarves, shawls, and nachaqs in the Nelson Island Diamond pattern.

Nightmute, according to the locals, formed as a village when the Yup'ik people started moving to Nelson Island. The village lost most of its residents in 1964 when many people relocated to the new village of Toksook Bay. Today, most residents spend the summers at a fish camp about twenty miles away.

Although the last qassiq (men's house) was abandoned in the 1970s, the people of Tununak perform traditional dances and continue many other Yup'ik customs.

Photo © James Barker, Fairbanks, Alaska. Used by permission.

Toksook Bay was established in 1964 and almost everyone from Nightmute moved to Toksook Bay at that time. Its location allowed access to an annual freighter ship, making it easier and cheaper to obtain commercial goods at this location than elsewhere on Nelson Island.

Newtok is north of Nelson Island across the Ninglick River. Water defines life in Newtok. As in many small villages in rural Alaska, houses do not have indoor plumbing. Water from a lake is processed in a treatment plant, and people haul water to their homes from a public storage tank or melt ice when the tank is empty or frozen. Water is also forcing the town to move to a new location. Winter temperatures in Alaska have risen 5 to 7 degrees over the past decades and surface air temperatures over the Arctic Ocean continue to rise. Throughout the state, Native Alaskans have noticed changes in the sea ice for some time. In some areas this is causing changes in the habits and migration of sea mammals. In other areas, such as at Newtok, it directly threatens coastal villages. The village is planning to relocate to higher ground because of beach erosion directly related to the climate change

When Edward Nelson visited Tununak in 1878, only six people were living there. In 1889 Jesuit missionaries accompanied a Russian trader on a trip to Tununak. The Jesuits stayed behind

Nelson Island		
	Nightmute	Toksook Bay
	(nite'-myoot)	(took'-sook or tuck'-sook)
Population	234	569
Location	18 miles (29 km) upriver from Toksook Bay 100 miles (161 km) west of Bethel	115 miles (185 km) northwest of Bethel 505 miles (813 km) west of Anchorage Across the river from Nunivak Island
Area (land)	97.0 square miles (251.2 sq km)	33.1 square miles (85.7 sq km)
Area (water)	4.6 square miles (11.9 sq km)	40.9 square miles (105.9 sq km)
Elevation	14 feet (4.3 m)	70 feet (21.3 m)
Climate	Maritime climate	Maritime climate
Precipitation	22 inches (55.9 cm) annual average	22 inches (55.9 cm) annual average
Snowfall	43 inches (109.2 cm) annual average	43 inches (109.2 cm) annual average

when the trader left and constructed a large building that housed a church, a school, and an apartment for the priests. The mission stayed open for only three years, but other missions on Nelson Island were more successful and Catholic influence spread across the island.

Water defines life in Newtok.

Water is also forcing the town

to move to a new location.

Nelson Island		
	Newtok	Tununak
	(noo'-tock)	(too-noo'-nuck))
Population	315	328
Location	94 miles (151 km) northwest of Bethel	115 miles (185 km) northwest of Bethel 519 miles (835 km) northwest of Anchorage
Area (land)	1.0 square mile (2.6 sq km)	60.5 square miles (156.7 sq km)
Area (water)	0.1 square mile (.26 sq km)	0.2 square mile (.52 sq km)
Elevation	25 feet (7.6 m)	70 feet (21.3 m)
Climate	Maritime climate	Maritime climate
Precipitation	17 inches (43.2 cm) annual average	17 inches (43.2 cm) annual average
Snowfall	22 inches (55.9 cm) annual average	28 inches (71.1 cm) annual average

Shishmaref and the Seward Peninsula

The Star design knitted in Shishmaref and on the Seward Peninsula is adapted from the beadwork on the tops of mukluks, or winter boots. This is a rare pattern.

Knitted in lightweight yarn. Photo by Bill Bacon, courtesy of Bill Bacon and Oomingmak Musk Ox Producers' Co-operative.

Shishmaref is located on Sarichef Island, in the Chukchi Sea off the northern shore of the Seward Peninsula. Seward Peninsula is the portion of Alaska that reaches out farthest into the Bering Sea toward Russia. Kigiktaq, the original Eskimo name for Sarichef Island, was inhabited for several hundred years before the arrival of Outsiders. A Russian explorer named Otto Von Kotzebue named an inlet near the village Shishmarev, after a member of his crew. Because it has an excellent harbor, Shishmaref became a key port for supplying gold-mining camps in the early twentieth century.

One hundred miles from Siberia, the island is now part of the Shared Beringia Heritage Program, established in 1991 as an international program between the Soviet Union and the United States. The program continues today as the governments of Russia and the United States work together with the Native people to protect the original residents' subsistence rights and activities, and to reestablish local cultural traditions and trade between the Natives of both nations.

As the northernmost village in the co-op, Shishmaref is most affected by the melting of polar ice. Sea ice forms a barrier that protects the land from erosion. As these ice packs become smaller, and during some winters do not form at all, coastal villages receive the brunt of storms from which they would have been protected in the past. Permafrost (land that stays frozen year-round) in Shishmaref is melting as well. Residents have decided to relocate the village by 2009, but the cost to do this is estimated at almost $200 million.

Shishmaref is located on a small island near Siberia. Before Russia sold Alaska to the United States, Native people from both sides of the International Date Line visited frequently, trading goods and participating in shared traditions and ceremonies.

The knitters in Shishmaref, and other knitters living on the Seward Peninsula, knit the Star pattern. The design is adapted from bead-work on the tops of mukluks, or winter boots. Shishmaref joined the co-op in 1971 and has had only 18 knitters since then; scarves and nachaqs with the Star pattern are both rare and desirable.

Shishmaref and the Seward Peninsula	
(shis'-muh'ref; soo'-ward; data are for Shishmaref)	
Population	581
Location	5 miles (8 km) from the mainland 126 miles (203 km) north of Nome 550 miles (885 km) northwest of Fairbanks
Area (land)	2.8 square miles (7.3 sq km)
Area (water)	4.5 square miles (11.7 sq km)
Elevation	20 feet (6.1 m)
Climate	Transitional climate, between arctic and subarctic with foggy summers. The Chukchi Sea normally freezes from mid-November to mid-June.
Precipitation	8 inches (20.3 cm) annual average
Snowfall	33 inches (83.8 cm) annual average

St. Mary's and Andreafsky

Only seven members have knitted the Dancers pattern since St. Mary's joined the co-op, making it one of the rare patterns. This interpretive design was adapted from the carving on a small ivory object from the eleventh or twelfth century.

Knitted in lightweight yarn. Photo by Bill Bacon, courtesy of Bill Bacon and Oomingmak Musk Ox Producers' Co-operative.

The city of St. Mary's includes two Yup'ik villages: St. Mary's and Andreafsky. Both villages are north of the Andreafsky River, 5 miles from where it joins the Yukon.

The St. Mary's mission school was originally 90 miles downriver from its current location at Akulurak, the "in-between place." In 1903 Catholic nuns opened the school to take care of children orphaned during the flu epidemic of 1900 to 1901 that decimated the area. The school became popular and by 1915 had seventy students. As was common at the time, students were not allowed to speak their native languages and were often not allowed visits from relatives. If they disobeyed the rules, students—both boys and girls—would be punished physically, frequently by lashing. In 1949 the village and mission moved to the current location, because buildings were beginning to sink into the soft tundra as the river changed its course. After relocating, St. Mary's became a well-respected boarding school with a high number of graduates going on to college until it closed in 1987.

Andreafsky was the site of a Russian Orthodox church built by the Andrea family. Originally a supply depot, the site was the winter headquarters for the Northern Commercial Company's fleet. The village was also home to the first commercial fishery on the Yukon River. After the St. Mary's mission moved in 1949, many Yup'ik families moved to Andreafsky. Andreafsky was annexed to St. Mary's in 1980.

The incorporated city of St. Mary's includes the villages of St. Mary's and Andreafsky.

Since 1980 the Andreafsky River has been a National Wild and Scenic River. Generally ice-free after the first of June, the Andreafsky River is used by local residents for subsistence fishing and hunting.

Co-op members from the villages of St. Mary's and Andreafsky knit the Dancers pattern. St. Mary's joined the co-op in 1970 and since then, seven knitters have worked the Dancers pattern.

St. Mary's (including Andreafsky)	
(an-dree-aff'-ski)	
Population	570 (145 in Andreafsky)
Location	450 miles (724 km) west-northwest of Anchorage
Area (land)	44.0 square miles (114 sq km)
Area (water)	6.3 square miles (16.3 sq km)
Elevation	311 feet (95 m)
Climate	Continental with maritime influence. The Andreafsky River normally freezes from November to June.
Precipitation	16 inches (40.6 cm) annual average
Snowfall	60 inches (152.4 cm) annual average

Marshall

The Woven Grass Basket design knitted in Marshall is made from yarn that is twice as thick as the yarn used in other scarves.

Knitted in heavier yarn. Photo by Bill Bacon, courtesy of Bill Bacon and Oomingmak Musk Ox Producers' Co-operative.

Named for Thomas Riley Marshall, the United States vice president under Woodrow Wilson, this village has been known by many names through its history and as its population has flowed and ebbed. Called Uglovaia ("little bow") when an expedition came to the village in 1880, the local residents also remember the village being called Maserculiq, "the place to catch spawning salmon." The small Yup'ik village turned into a gold rush town after gold was discovered nearby in 1913. The town became known as Marshall's Landing because it was easy to reach by riverboat. (The village itself is actually eight miles downriver from the landing.)

A post office was opened in 1915 when the population grew to over a thousand. According to the U.S. Post Office, the village was called Fortuna Ledge after the first child born in the mining camp, Fortuna Hunter. Fortuna Hunter herself, on the other hand, claims that she was named after the town when she was born in 1916. She says that when the village applied for a zip code, the Postal Service required the town to choose a new name because there was already a city named Marshall in Alabama. According to Hunter, the miners chose the name Fortuna Ledge because they'd had good fortune in the area. Both names—Fortuna Ledge and Marshall—were used until 1984, when the town officially became Marshall. By then it was common for cities in different states to share the same name (or it was at least more obvious that this frequently occurred).

Today, the community has returned to its roots and is once again a Yup'ik village. Most residents rely on subsistence

Alaska

Marshall

Marshall, at one time a gold rush town with more than 1,000 residents, is near two gold mines that can be reached using all-terrain vehicles.

activities to feed their families with salmon, moose, bear, and waterfowl. Seasonal work in fishing, fish processing, and firefighting provides cash.

Marshall joined the co-op in 1971 and has had twenty-four knitters making heavy-weight scarves in a lace pattern inspired by the design of grass baskets woven in the village.

Marshall	
Population	370
Location	75 miles (121 km) north of Bethel 400 miles (644 km) west-northwest of Anchorage
Area (land)	4.7 square miles (12.2 sq km)
Elevation	103 feet (31.4 m)
Climate	Maritime. The lower Yukon River normally freezes from November to mid-June.
Precipitation	16 inches (40.6 cm) annual average

Aleutian Islands

The Aleutian Islands, extending from the southwest coast of Alaska, separate the Pacific Ocean from the Bering Sea. Like the Hawaiian Islands, the Aleutians rise sharply out of the sea with dangerous shores, steep mountains, and several active volcanoes.

Closely related to the Alaskan Eskimos, the Unangax^ people, often called Aleuts (ah'-lee-yoots), moved to the islands from the mainland thousands of years ago. Settling in areas near both the sea and sources of fresh water, they were able to protect their lands against invasion from other Native Alaskans while having easy access to salmon and other food sources.

The Aleutians were the first part of Alaska to be visited by the Russians when, in 1741, explorers encountered the islands. Soon after, Russian hunters and fur traders overran the land. The people of the Aleutians were almost wiped out through slaughter, slavery, and disease as the Russians expanded their influence in the area.

Russian Orthodox churches became the main structures in most villages, and the faith remains a strong Aleutian influence to this day.

Photo © Alaska Division of Tourism. Used by permission.

Part of the volcanic "ring of fire" surrounding the Pacific, the 1,100-mile-long Aleutian archipelago is rocky and almost treeless.

During the time of Russian domination, the Aleutian population fell from 25,000 to less than 2,000. Unlike the Yup'ik and Inupiat cultures, much of the Aleut way of life was destroyed. In 1867, Russia sold the Aleutian Islands to the United States with the rest of Alaska.

The Japanese occupied the Aleutians during World War II. With the western-most island only 500 miles from Asia, and much farther from any city in the continental United States, the area was vulnerable to attack. During the Aleutian Campaign, many Unangax^ were sent to internment camps in other parts of Alaska, and their homes and villages were burned to stop the Japanese from taking them. In the camps, as many as 10 percent of the detainees died. In 1996 Congress established the Aleutian World War II National Historic Area to recognize and commemorate the contributions of the people of the Aleutian Islands during the war.

Today Unalaska and Dutch Harbor are the major population centers in the Aleutians and the area is home to the state's largest fishing fleet. The islands are also the site of research stations and U.S. military bases.

Knitters from the Aleutian Islands first joined the Oomingmak Co-op in 1978, and to date there have been nine knitters making the unique and beautiful Seal Hunt and Sea Urchin patterns.

Aleutian Islands	
(ah-loo'-shun)	
Population	8,162 on the entire archipelago 4,283 in Unalaska
Location	Southwest of mainland Alaska, extending 1,100 miles (1,770 km) into the Pacific Ocean
Elevation	Some areas are at sea level; the volcano Makushin is 5,905 feet (1,800 m)
Climate	Oceanic with relatively steady temperatures and heavy rainfall
Precipitation	80 inches (203.2 cm) Said to be the rainiest place in the United States.

Dominic Cotignola

New knitters and villages

The Tundra and Snow line is the newest addition to the products made by the members of Oomingmak Musk Ox Producers' Co-operative.

To start the Tundra and Snow line, the co-op recruited new knitters from around the state of Alaska.

According to Sigrun Robertson, director of the Oomingmak Co-op, when a new village is interested in joining the group, "We go out to the village and do a one- or two-day workshop for interested knitters, such as we have done the last few years in the following villages: Aleknagik, Eagle, Ekwok, New Stuyahok, Koliganek, Goodnews Bay, Stebbins, and Gambell. We had a grant from the Catholic Campaign of Human Development to recruit more women in villages where we had not been before. We sent out letters to village councils and advertised in the local papers, and then responded to the villages that showed interest in having us come out. We explain about the co-op and how it works, show the various items that they can make, and get them started filling out membership papers, and [we] start them working on their swatch[es]."

Sigrun Robertson explains what happens when a knitter from one of the member villages wants to begin knitting for the co-op: "If a request to join comes in the mail, often from a family member or friend of a current member, we send them the membership papers and the pattern for the test swatch by mail. Once they have signed the papers and proven by their test [swatch] that they are capable knitters, we get them started with one or two of the regular pieces."

Alaska

Tips for visiting rural Alaska

During my trip to Alaska, I was able to visit only one Eskimo village, Unalakleet. Most of the villages in rural Alaska have no accommodations for visitors. With more than 600 residents, Unalakleet is one of the largest Eskimo villages in Alaska. Because the village has two lodges, visitors can stay without inconveniencing anyone. When the co-op sets up a workshop in a small community, many times the visitors sleep on the floor at the public school or in the homes of community members. Although many writers will go to the ends of the earth to pursue their research, I did not want to impose on any of the co-op knitters by intruding in their communities and lives.

Dominic Cotignola

If you intend to visit rural Alaska, please keep these things in mind:

▸ The only way in or out of most rural towns is by plane, and few villages have accommodations for tourists.

▸ Respect the privacy and culture of the people you meet. In the past, planes of tourists and photographers landed in villages, the tourists got out, took photos, got back on the plane, and left. Today, the residents of many small villages are understandably leery of unannounced visitors.

▸ Be sure to check state and local regulations if you intend to fish or hunt. Don't trespass if you are hiking, fishing, or hunting. Signs are seldom posted to distinguish between public and private land so make sure you know where you are welcome.

▸ The knitters of the Oomingmak Co-op remain anonymous to protect their privacy. If you want to meet co-op members, contact the store in Anchorage. Several members work there and would be happy to talk to you.

Viewing musk oxen

The Musk Ox Farm in Palmer, about an hour's drive from downtown Anchorage, is definitely worth visiting if you are in Alaska between Mother's Day and the end of September. Tours of the farm run every half hour and take you right up to the pens where the musk oxen live. Out of season, tours are available by appointment.

You can see adult males and females, yearlings, and calves. The farm also has a gift shop and interpretive center, with a musk ox hide and skulls that you can touch, as well as many photographs of animals and knitters from Oomingmak Musk Ox Producers' Co-operative. The tour guides provide an informative and entertaining discussion about the biology of musk oxen and about the ongoing experiment of domesticating these arctic animals. (Visit the farm's web site at www.muskoxfarm.org.)

The Large Animal Research Station (LARS) is the best place to view musk oxen if you are visiting Fairbanks. Like the Musk Ox Farm, LARS offers tours throughout the summer season. The tour guides at LARS have backgrounds in the natural sciences and provide descriptions of the animals' natural history and arctic adaptations. They also supply information about research on managing wild herds in an age of climate change and about increasing pressure to drill for oil in the musk oxen's habitat. LARS also has herds of caribou and reindeer. (Visit the LARS web site at www.uaf.edu/lars.)

A trip to view musk oxen in the wild can be expensive—and unsuccessful. If I had the time and the money, I would definitely take the risk. I can't imagine anything more exciting than seeing these creatures roaming wild in the Arctic. Most wild herds of musk oxen in Alaska live in areas that are accessible only by air, such as Nunivak and Nelson Islands and the Seward Peninsula, near Nome in western Alaska, and on the coastal plain of the Arctic National Wildlife Refuge in the northern part of the state. For the best chance of seeing musk oxen in the wild, visit Nome, where the animals are often seen along the side of the road. Contact the Nome Convention and Visitors Bureau and ask about their new ecotourism plans for promoting musk ox viewing.

Photos by Dominic Cotignola

Musk oxen at the Musk Ox Farm, in Palmer, Alaska.

Chapter 4

Musk oxen in Alaska

I couldn't view any musk oxen in the wild on my visit to Alaska. Alaska is so large that almost every trip requires an overnight stay or a plane ride, so the costs add up quickly. Luckily, both Fairbanks and Anchorage have captive musk ox herds nearby.

Under a blanket of snow in winter, musk oxen look like giant boulders forming lumps on the otherwise featureless terrain. Only when one of the boulders moves do you get a hint that animals covered with long, flowing brown hair have been resting under the snow. Even in summer, musk oxen move so slowly that they often look more like boulders than animals when seen from a distance. With its thick, insulating coat, slow metabolism, and sedentary lifestyle, the musk ox is ideally suited to the Far North.

Prehistoric origins

Musk oxen have roamed the earth for millions of years. First evolving in Asia during the Pliocene epoch (1.8 to 5.3 million years ago), many species of musk oxen dispersed into Europe and later into North America, crossing the Bering Land Bridge to Alaska from Siberia.

Although musk oxen survive today only in arctic and subarctic environments, their range was much greater before the last ice age. During the Pleistocene epoch (10,000 to 1.8 million years ago),

Dominic Cotignola

Reminiscent of the woolly mammoth, the much smaller musk ox seems to be a relic of prehistoric times.

musk oxen, along with mammoths and mastodons, moved south as the ice sheets spread across the Northern Hemisphere. Fossils of several species of musk oxen have been found as far south as France and Texas. Only one species of musk ox, *Ovibos moschatus*, survived from the last ice age to modern times.

Like sheep and goats, musk oxen are ruminants. With four-chambered stomachs, ruminants can digest a wide range of plants. After chewing and swallowing willow leaves, grass, or moss, musk oxen most often lie down for a leisurely cud-chewing session. An amusing side effect of this digestive process is that they burp continually.

Arctic adaptations

The home of the musk ox has short summers and cold, dark winters. Coming from a temperate climate, I often imagined their habitat as a barren and white arctic environment. I have since learned that snowfall is usually light, measuring only about 6 inches (15 cm) per year in many areas. Musk oxen cannot survive in areas with deep snow. They are able to scrape a thin layer of snow and ice away from underlying plants with their hooves, but they are not able to reach food under deep snow.

Dominic Cotignola

Musk oxen do not hibernate or migrate during winter. Instead, they have developed several adaptations perfectly suited to their environment. Their most noticeable protection against cold and wind is their long, shaggy hair. With two layers—long outer guard hairs and soft, downy underwool—their coats are similar to those of other animals that evolved in severe climates, including camels, vicuñas, and cashmere goats. The outer guard hairs never stop growing and can reach lengths of 2 feet (61 cm) on animals four years of age or older. These stiff hairs protect musk oxen from sun, wind, and insects—even during the summer after their

Musk oxen have two-toed hooves, horns that continue to grow throughout their lifetimes, and a coat of hair that can be used to spin yarn. In these ways, they resemble many types of sheep and goats. Because they don't shed completely, they develop thick, shaggy manes over the years.

downy undercoats shed. The down, called qiviut, creates a thick layer of insulation so effective that after a snowstorm the animals have to shake themselves free of snow. Even though body temperature for a musk ox is about 101 degrees F (38 degrees C), not enough body heat escapes to melt the snow and ice on its body. In fact, if a musk ox gets caught napping in wet, icy weather, it may become frozen to the ground.

Qiviut covers the entire body of the musk ox except for its nose, lips, eyes, and hooves. The long guard hairs and fluffy qiviut often hide the animals' tails and ears, making it "impossible to tell which end is the head," according to the first published account of these strange animals, written by Nicolas Jérémie. Their short legs are also protected by a layer of qiviut and are often almost invisible when the guard hairs, reaching their full length, form a skirt that extends almost to the ground. The guard hairs appear even longer during winter when the undercoat fibers are as much as 6 inches (15 cm) long on adults. (See Chapter 6 for more information on qiviut fiber and yarn.)

Musk oxen have developed several other adaptations to the cold. With males averaging 650 to 900 pounds (300 to 400 kg) and females averaging 450 to 600 pounds (200 to 275 kg), their stocky bodies help them retain heat. Brown fat stored in their shoulders gives them humps similar to those on camels. The fat reserves generate body heat in winter when food is scarce. Even calves have brown fat, which is especially advantageous to those born in early April when the weather is still quite cold.

Musk oxen spend most of their time lying down, chewing their cuds. This sedentary lifestyle allows them to conserve energy and burn few calories. During the winter, they are so still they are said to be in "standing hibernation." During fall and spring, the calves play in the refreshing, cool weather, but the adults seldom exert themselves and almost never run. Although musk oxen can

Dominic Cotignola

With 5 to 6 pounds (2.3 to 2.7 kg) of qiviut on each animal, musk oxen look larger than their bodies are, just as unshorn sheep or long-haired cats do. Musk oxen in the wild have longer and more pointed horns, as you can see on page 70.

run very fast for short distances, when facing predators they form a defensive circle. The adults face outward, exposing their large horns to scare off wolves or bears. This strategy prevents them from overheating and protects the calves that are hidden in the center of the circle.

Musk oxen are not good at dealing with warm weather and they overheat in temperatures as low as 70 degrees F (21 degrees C). They pant like dogs to cool off, although they do have sweat glands. During the summer, they often lie in snow banks and stand in streams to keep cool.

Behavior

Musk oxen are social animals, gathering in small herds, usually of ten to twenty animals. A herd normally stays within a small area during the summer and may join other herds to form groups of up to seventy-five animals during the winter. Sometimes as many as two hundred animals travel together for a short time. When the food supply no longer supports the population, the herd splits into smaller groups which may move as far as two hundred miles away in search of new habitat.

Each herd follows a strict hierarchy, with dominant males having access to the females for mating. Adult males compete in fierce head-butting contests to prove their strength. With huge horns and large horny bosses on their foreheads, the crack of a collision sounds like thunder in the quiet arctic setting as males run together from distances of up to 50 yards (46 m) at full speed. The display is repeated until one bull backs down, is injured, or, occasionally, dies from head injuries. Although their thick skulls and bosses offer some protection, bulls generally have shorter lifespans than females due to this violent behavior.

Females also have horns, which are much smaller and join on their foreheads underneath a cover of hair. Calves start growing horns in the first summer, and the horns reach full size at three years of age for females and six years for males.

Dominic Cotignola

Musk ox calves grow quickly, reaching up to ten times their birth weight in the first year.

Musk oxen don't mate in spring as most animals do. Because of the harsh conditions in which they live, most female musk oxen mate only once every two years. They breed in fall and their calves are born between April and June of the following year. This timing gives the babies an opportunity to grow a layer of insulating qiviut before the hazardous winter weather sets in. Weighing only 20 to 30 pounds (9 to 13.5 kg), a calf can hide invisibly under its mother's long guard-hair skirt. A mother will often not wean a calf from her milk, which has the consistency of heavy cream, until the calf is over a year old.

Native Alaskans

Caribou, seals, walrus, and whales were the mammals most prized by the Eskimos of Alaska and the Inuits of Canada. However, when these were scarce, musk oxen often provided substitute raw material for an assortment of products.

Musk ox meat, while not a favorite food, was sometimes easier to come by than caribou, because caribou herds frequently migrate to distant feeding grounds as the seasons change. Musk oxen also retain body fat throughout the year. This necessary part of the arctic diet would have been welcome during the lean months of late winter or early spring when other animals are often thin. Although musk ox fat smokes more than seal oil when it burns, it can be used as fuel in a pinch.

As with other land and marine mammals, the bones and horns of musk oxen were well suited to being carved into tools and utensils such as needle cases, ladles, and skin scrapers. The horns also provided material for decorative items such as toggles on clothing, pipe stems, and closures on skin or grass bags. Musk ox skins could substitute for walrus- or sealskin for making bedding, tents, and clothing, but because the thick hair is quite flammable and the qiviut is easily soiled, it was never used for these purposes unless the other materials were not available.

Sometimes the hair was removed from the skins and used for other purposes. The long, stiff guard hairs could be twisted, like sinew, into strong thread and string to make small nets for collecting bird eggs and mosquito masks to protect against Alaska's ubiquitous pests. Qiviut occasionally served as insulation and as decoration on masks, but before the arrival of Outsiders spinning and knitting were unknown in Alaska and this soft fiber was not used to make fabric for clothing.

European explorers

In 1689 Henry Kelsey was the first European to see a musk ox. When he encountered a curious "buffalo" as he led the first European exploration of the Canadian interior, he wrote about it in his journal. The animal's horns, he wrote, "joyn together on their forehead, and so come down ye side of their head, and turned up till ye tips be even with ye buts."

It was over thirty years before anyone published a description of a musk ox. In 1720 Nicolas Jérémie, the governor of a French fort on Hudson Bay, published his description of the *boeuf musqué,* or "musk cattle." Based on the appearance and smell of the

Reading about Arctic explorers

During my visit to Alaska, Fran Degnan, a knitter and lifelong resident of Unalakleet, suggested that I read *Ada Blackjack,* by Jennifer Niven. Ada Blackjack was Fran Degnan's aunt, and her story is fascinating. In 1921 she volunteered to accompany an Arctic expedition to serve as seamstress to a group of young, inexperienced explorers. Intending to hire an entire team of Eskimo guides and hunters, the explorers were unsuccessful at recruiting anyone but Ada, who took the job because she desperately needed money to care for her sick son.

Vilhjalmur Stefansson, the Canadian-American Arctic explorer who planned this expedition, was smitten with musk oxen from the first time he saw the woolly creatures. During one expedition, he and his crew ate musk ox meat and burned both the tallow and the hair of the animals for fuel. They also constructed a house-sized tent from musk ox hides. During a single expedition in 1916 and 1917, Stefansson's team killed almost 400 musk oxen. Undoubtedly the men would have frozen to death or died of starvation without this source of food and shelter, because they were stranded for a year in the arctic with only four months of supplies, due to poor planning and unanticipated problems.

Unfortunately, not all of Stefansson's expeditions were so lucky. Believing that the "friendly Arctic" was as hospitable as more temperate areas, Stefansson was sometimes sloppy in planning and managing his expeditions. In several cases he sent a crew of young men with no experienced leaders to remote and frigid locations in the Arctic, places that were so barren that not even Eskimos attempted to live there. On one such ill-fated expedition, Ada Blackjack was the only person to survive. Two years after being stranded on Wrangle Island, off the coast of Russia, with no means of obtaining additional supplies or rations, she was rescued. She had spent the previous winter teaching herself to hunt while she watched her last teammate die of scurvy.

I was amazed to learn that Vilhjalmur Stefansson was the first person to suggest domesticating musk oxen. He thought the animals would be an excellent source of food and fiber and that they could be commercially exploited to the advantage of indigenous peoples of the Far North. He was never able to implement a musk ox domestication program, but his ideas influenced the founding of the Oomingmak Co-op and of the Musk Ox Farm.

animals, Jérémie thought they were cattle with musk glands. He was wrong on both counts, but the name stuck and remains in use today in French, English, and other languages.

Nicolas Jérémie introduced qiviut to France, and considered the fiber to be more luxurious than silk and longer than the wool of African Barbary sheep. He had stockings knitted from the qiviut, and recommended that the fiber be studied for possible commercial uses.

Most explorers and whalers hunted musk oxen for food. At times they killed entire herds to butcher just a few animals. Explorers also fed musk ox meat to their sled dogs. The defensive formation of musk oxen, which worked so well against their natural predators, did little to protect them from men with rifles. Hunters would send dogs to frighten the musk ox herd into its circular formation, and then they would shoot every animal within a few minutes. These explorers also killed entire herds of musk oxen to capture a few calves for zoos.

During the late nineteenth century, as bison were becoming scarce, Hudson's Bay Company started producing musk ox robes. Between 1862 and 1916, the company purchased over 17,000 skins to make carriage robes. Hudson's Bay Company also sold approximately 1,100 pounds (500 kg) of qiviut.

Whalers and explorers may have used the down to stuff mattresses or sleeping bags, or even to pack fragile items for shipping, but there are no records of knitted or woven qiviut items produced or sold.

Conservation

By the end of the nineteenth century, musk oxen were extinct in Alaska and their numbers were drastically reduced in Canada and Greenland. During the same period, musk ox populations on Arctic islands also dropped significantly, although this change was not due to hunting.

The Northwest Game Act of 1917 prohibited hunting in Canada except by indigenous peoples in danger of starvation. The act was amended in 1924 to prohibit all hunting. With hunting pressure removed, musk ox herds in Canada began to increase, first gradually and then dramatically. Today, Canada has more than 125,000 musk oxen and Inuits are once again able to hunt them in limited numbers. Primarily interested in the meat, the people of Nunivak and Inuvak sell qiviut from musk ox carcasses to commercial yarn manufacturers in Canada and Peru.

Musk oxen were reintroduced to Alaska when thirty-four animals were captured in Greenland in 1930 and began an eight-thousand–mile journey by ship, train, and barge that would ultimately last almost six years. When the animals finally reached Alaska, they spent five years at a research facility in Fairbanks before finally going to their new home on Nunivak Island.

The herd thrived on Nunivak, and soon outgrew the available food sources. From those original thirty-four musk oxen, Alaska now has almost four thousand animals living on Nunivak and Nelson Islands, on the Seward Peninsula, in the Arctic National Wildlife Refuge, and in northwest Alaska.

When musk oxen were reintroduced to Alaska, it was without the consent or advice of the people living in the areas where the animals were released. Many local people were, and still are, afraid of these imposing and unfamiliar creatures. Yup'ik and Inupiat residents in some areas feel that the reintroduced musk oxen are taking habitat away from caribou, a traditional food source. This conflict causes continuous disagreement as well as some poaching of musk

oxen by discontented residents of rural villages who feel that their aboriginal land rights are ignored by state and federal governments.

Today there are 150,000 wild musk oxen around the world. This success may not, however, be the end of the story. With a low tolerance for heat, musk oxen are at risk of losing their last remnant of habitat as global climate change causes the Arctic to warm nearly twice as fast as the rest of the planet. The animals are also intolerant of human encroachment into their territory and have been known to charge at low-flying aircraft, leaping off the ground in attempts to attack the noisy trespassers. With increased pressure to drill for oil in Alaska, the land of the musk ox may once again lose this ancient, Arctic mammal to man's advance.

Only if we follow Yup'ik and Inupiat tradition and deliberately choose to preserve our natural environment for future generations will the musk ox survive.

Musk oxen form a defensive circle when they feel threatened.

John J. Teal Jr. was fascinated by the idea of domesticating musk oxen. He thought that musk oxen would soon be extinct in the wild, and that domestication was the only way to preserve the species. Fortunately, he was wrong.

Photo by Jimmy Bedford, courtesy of Oomingmak Musk Ox Producers' Co-operative.

Chapter 5

A new venture: The beginning of the co-op

Everywhere I went in Alaska, it seemed that I heard another story about John Teal. Everyone involved in the early days of the Oomingmak Co-op knew him and it soon became clear that his passion was at the heart of the project at its inception.

An anthropology graduate and football player from Harvard University, Teal met the Arctic explorer Vilhjalmur Stefansson in the 1940s. Stefansson, who believed that "musk oxen can make a square mile of arctic tundra as valuable as sheep can a square mile of Alberta," was the first person to promote domestication of the musk ox.

Handling musk oxen

John Teal believed that musk ox domestication could be a tool for bringing financial security to Native Alaskan communities and, in 1954, he founded the Institute of Northern Agricultural Research (INAR). With three calves captured from the Thelon Wildlife Sanctuary in Canada and four more captured later, Teal established a musk ox farm in Vermont.

While the experimental farm provided experience in raising musk oxen and processing qiviut, the most important part of the project was the new technique Teal developed for capturing calves. Instead of frightening the herd into their circular defensive posture and shooting the adults to capture the calves as early explorers had done, Teal used planes to chase down the animals and drive them into the water. Once in the water, it was easy to separate the mothers from their calves. Nonetheless, capturing even a small musk ox required stength and stamina.

On the Vermont farm, the animals were combed every year when they began to shed qiviut. Teal never considered shearing them because he'd heard of a young musk ox in the Bronx Zoo that had been sheared and died of pneumonia.

Teal dreamed of raising the animals in their native environment. After the ten-year experiment in Vermont, he wanted to start a full-sized domestication project in Alaska.

In 1964, with funding from the W. K. Kellogg Foundation, John Teal got approval from the University of Alaska to establish a farm

Qiviut: Early studies of the fiber

Most people who saw sheared qiviut, laden with thick, prickly guard hairs, thought it would be too expensive and labor intensive to remove the guard hairs to obtain a commercially viable luxury fiber. To test that hypothesis, Stefansson collected about 50 pounds (23 kg) of qiviut from musk ox carcasses and divided it among the National Bureau of Standards in the United States, several Canadian fiber manufacturers, and Professor Aldred F. Barker, head of the textiles department at the University of Leeds in England.

In June 1922, F. H. Atkinson published the Leeds findings in his doctoral thesis, "Ovibos Fibre." Although Atkinson found qiviut to be "of such delicious softness that it can be favorably compared to cashmere and vicuña," he was discouraged by the labor involved in removing the guard hairs. He concluded that "it was well nigh impossible to sort out all the coarse outer hair, and it would certainly not appear to be a commercial proposition to do so." Today the successful production of sumptuous qiviut yarn from combed animals in Alaska and sheared hides in Canada proves that Atkinson was wrong.

The researchers at Leeds blended some of the qiviut with coarse wool, so the resulting yarn was not nearly as soft as the 100 percent qiviut yarn available today. The qiviut/wool blend was woven into suiting fabric and sewn into suits for King George V, Stefansson, and Barker. (Stefansson's suit

was lost when his wife cleaned the closet and gave the suit that her husband never wore to the Salvation Army.)

In the 1930s, two more studies were conducted on qiviut processing and production.

The first study was conducted by Werner von Bergen, chief chemist at Forstmann Woolen Company. Published just two years after the musk oxen were brought to Alaska from Greenland, von Bergen's study was meticulously detailed and conducted under strict scientific conditions. After examining fibers under a microscope and comparing qiviut to mohair, alpaca, yak, vicuña, cashmere, and camel, von Bergen decided that qiviut compared best to cashmere. He concluded that, with the domestication of the musk ox in Alaska, "the finest quality of the finest dress goods will be manufactured by Americans from an American product."

The second study was less formal and more productive. Lydia Fohn-Hansen, founder of the Fairbanks Weavers' and Spinners' Guild and head of the home economics department at the University of Alaska in Fairbanks, experimented with fiber processing, weaving, and knitting. Working with handspun yarn, Fohn-Hansen's students wove and sold scarves until 1934, when the thirty-two animals were released on Nunivak Island because the project's funding ran out. This experiment showed that a cottage industry selling handmade qiviut garments was a real possibility.

Dominic Cotignola

Young musk oxen adapt readily to handling and the farm routine.

on university land. With permits from the Alaska Department of Fish and Game and the U.S. Fish and Wildlife Service, he was ready to capture calves on Nunivak Island. During expeditions in 1965 and 1966, he found it more difficult to capture calves on the island than it had been in Canada. With patience, the team eventually captured thirty-two calves and transported them to their new home in Fairbanks.

Just as in Vermont, the young animals adapted readily to handling and the farm routine. With daily weighing and feeding, they became familiar with their human captors and were easily led into stalls when it was time to comb out the qiviut in spring. The animals thrived in Fairbanks, and the first captive calves were born in 1967. To encourage the females to breed every year, instead of every other year as in the wild, the babies were weaned after several months. By 1975 the herd numbered over 100.

Challenging times

In the mid-1970s, the farm at Fairbanks began having problems with overgrazing and calf mortality. John Teal was also experiencing conflict with the authorities at the University of Alaska. His freewheeling style did not fit the structure of a university research center. Teal's focus was on domesticating musk oxen and producing qiviut; the biologists wanted to conduct formal studies on musk ox behavior and biology. Teal, an anthropologist, did not have the respect of the biologists; he, in turn, did not respect their research methods. This schism in purpose continues today, with the Musk Ox Farm focusing on domestication, qiviut production, and tourism, and the Large Animal Research Station emphasizing biological and behavioral research.

Teal's original goal had been for the Fairbanks herd to seed new herds that would be owned and managed by Native Alaskans in their home villages. With the problems in Fairbanks, it was impossible to start new herds and continue the existing farm at the same time. Teal decided to move the entire herd to Unalakleet, the

Dominic Cotignola

For ten years, the Musk Ox Farm found a home in Unalakleet.

Inupiat village located 395 miles (635 km) northwest of Anchorage. This move would not only meet the goal of having a musk ox herd under the control of an Eskimo village, it would also relocate the musk oxen to an environment closer to their natural habitat.

Transporting more than 100 bulky, ornery animals to Unalakleet—accessible only by plane—was no easy task, and maintaining the herd in this remote location proved to be no easier than it had been in Fairbanks. Not everyone in Unalakleet was happy with the new neighbors. The site chosen for the farm was in a prime berry-picking location, and many residents were also afraid of the lumbering animals with imposing horns.

While the herd size remained stable in Unalakleet, obtaining enough food to keep the animals from starving during the winter was almost impossible. Unalakleet does not get much snowfall, but strong winds bring snow from the inland hills to the village and the drifts can grow to more than 15 feet (4.6 m). While musk oxen can tolerate cold, they can't dig through deep snow to find food. In 1980, 15,000 bales of hay were mailed to Unalakleet to feed the animals. The cost itself was prohibitive; even worse, the Postal Service refused to ship any more hay after its machinery filled with fodder. Following intense negotiations, the postmaster general finally agreed to allow the hay shipments to continue as long as each bale was packaged in a way that would prevent hay from getting into the postal equipment.

With the local controversy over the presence of these strange animals, the difficulty of keeping them fed during the winter, and the high cost of sending bales of hay by airmail, the fate of the herd was once again unsure.

As beautiful as it is, the Matanuska River Valley is not musk ox terrain.

Soon the animals were on their way back to an urban area. After a short stay on the Susitna Ranch near Talkeetna, the herd found a permanent home in Palmer. The 75-acre farm was originally part of an agricultural colony founded by President Roosevelt after the Depression. The valley was home to 203 families from the Midwest who relocated to Alaska in 1935 to establish farms. In the days when meat, milk, and vegetables were locally produced, these farms provided fresh food as the population exploded. Although the area is becoming a suburb of Anchorage, it remains bucolic and seems to hang in the past. Many of the original barns are still standing, in various states of disrepair. The peaceful valley, with the Alaskan mountains in the background, seems the perfect place for small farms.

In 1975 Helen Howard, who worked with the Oomingmak Co-op at its inception, wrote, "Teal's work with musk oxen has demonstrated beyond reasonable doubt the feasibility of commercial musk ox farming." Yet, unfortunately, the early successes have not been sustained.

As beautiful as it is, the Matanuska River Valley is not musk ox terrain. For reasons that are still not completely understood, the herd size has been shrinking. In 1992 sixty-seven animals remained; today there are only forty. Unless the problems with disease and calf mortality can be solved, the fate of the musk ox domestication project is uncertain, at best. With the shrinking size of the herd, the qiviut harvest has also decreased. Today, most qiviut yarn is spun from fiber harvested from animals hunted in Canada. In 2000, for the first time, the Oomingmak Co-op made a one-time purchase of qiviut from Canada to use in their new Tundra and Snow items.

A knitting cottage industry

While John Teal worked on the farm with the animals, combing and saving the qiviut every spring, Ann Lillian Schell and Helen Howard were doing the foundation work on a plan to set up a knitting co-op-

The Musk Ox Farm is in the Matanuska River Valley, the agricultural center of Alaska.

Dominic Cotignola

erative. The two worked with Dorothy Reade, a spinner and knitter from Eugene, Oregon, to develop lace stitches and charts for the co-op's first lace scarf pattern.

In 1961 Dorothy Reade had written to the University of Alaska Co-operative Extension Service seeking information on sources for qiviut fiber. The extension service referred her to John Teal, who was raising musk oxen in Vermont at the time. It took a few years, but finally—in 1965—Dorothy Reade received a pound of qiviut from John Teal, who was by then in Alaska. She was to experiment with the fiber and report back to the University of Alaska with her recommendations on how the fiber could be used commercially. A pound is a lot of qiviut.

After removing the guard hairs from the qiviut using tweezers, Reade spun several qiviut yarns, including blends with wool, silk, and Dacron, and then knitted sample garments.

As she told Helen Howard and Ann Lillian Schell at a knitting workshop in 1968, qiviut alone does not have the strength or memory to hold its shape in fitted garments such as sweaters, mittens, and socks. Dorothy Reade suggested blends for making garments (such as the qiviut/wool/silk blend I used to knit the Grass-Basket Cropped Ruana Vest on page 146). Pure qiviut is

The first knitting workshop in Mekoryuk was a success, and more than twenty women learned to knit lace with qiviut yarn.

The first workshop, courtesy of Oomingmak Musk Ox Producers' Co-operative.

Helen Howard (above, on right) and Ann Lillian Schell (above far right) taught knitting workshops in villages across Alaska.

Photos courtesy of Oomingmak Musk Ox Producers' Co-operative. Photo of Ann Lillian Schell, blocking a scarf, by Jimmy Bedford.

better used in scarves, shawls, and other items that emphasize its soft drape and do not require elasticity in the yarn.

Dorothy Reade had developed an easy-to-follow system for charting knitting patterns. Frustrated by the complicated line-by-line instructions used in most of the knitting books of the time, she created her own system for "drawing" the knitting on a grid. Each square on the grid looked like the stitch created with the needles.

This system was perfectly suited to the new knitters of the Oomingmak Musk Ox Producers' Co-operative, because many of them spoke only Yup'ik or Inupiat, and, although many were already expert knitters they wouldn't have been able to follow instructions written in English.

In 1967 there was finally enough qiviut to send to a cashmere mill for processing. After yarn was spun, it was time to start finding knitters.

In December 1968, Ann Lillian Schell went to Mekoryuk on Nunivak Island to teach a knitting workshop using the techniques she had learned from Dorothy Reade. Like my short trip to Unalakleet, Ann Schell's trip to Mekoryuk didn't work out as planned.

She planned to visit the village for a week, to work with the knitters in formal workshops, and to get each knitter started on a scarf in the Harpoon pattern. She took instruction sheets, yarn, and knitting needles to hand out in the workshops. The materials were neatly packed in plastic bags, one kit for each student. The yarn was provided free of charge to the knitters, but the needles cost fifty cents a pair.

After corresponding with the Village Council, everything was arranged for the beginning of December. The weather did not cooperate, however, and after several delays, Ann Schell arrived in Mekoryuk on the mail plane on December 20, just in time for Christmas. With holiday festivities in full swing, the scheduled workshops were out of the question.

After settling in the school guest room, the only available accommodation during the busy holiday season, Schell met a group of girls at a 4-H meeting and asked them to tell their mothers that she had finally arrived. That night, sitting on the floor in the school guest room, surrounded by two or three knitters at a time, she patiently showed each one how to read the lace charts and to convert the rows of Xs, Os, and Bs on the charts into knitted lace. Because many of the knitters did not speak English, most of the lesson was spent pointing to the symbol on the chart, and then working the stitch to show the knitters that the symbols looked like the knitted stitches. The experienced knitters in the group caught on quickly.

The next day, a second lesson was "scheduled" after a volleyball game, and several other impromptu meetings were held at homes throughout the week. A few young girls who didn't know how to knit came to some of the meetings. Ann Schell showed them how to knit and purl and encouraged them to practice for a while before trying anything more complicated.

Knitters practicing with qiviut during a workshop in Tununak, on Nelson Island.

Photo by Bill Bacon, courtesy of Oomingmak Musk Ox Producers' Co-operative.

Private musk ox farms

Today, while there are over 150,000 wild musk oxen worldwide, there are only a few hundred domestic animals. In addition to the Musk Ox Farm and LARS, several universities, zoos, and private farms have captive musk oxen. Two private farms have produced qiviut yarn.

At the Musk Ox Company in Hamilton, Montana, Nancy and Joel Bender began raising musk oxen in 1993. At first they handspun the fiber combed from their animals; later they developed a successful commercial line of qiviut yarn sold under the MOCO Yarns label. After well over a decade, they sold their animals to farms in Alaska and Canada, as well as to several zoos.

Today, Windy Valley Muskox, a farm owned by Dianne and John Nash in Palmer, has a small herd of eleven musk oxen. The original three animals came from the Benders' Montana herd and the rest were born on the Nash farm. The Nashes sell fiber for spinning, combed from their own animals, in addition to qiviut yarn.

Musk oxen at Windy Valley Muskox.

Photo © John Nash. Used by permission.

On Christmas Eve and Christmas Day, everyone took time off from knitting. During her stay in Mekoryuk, Ann Schell was graciously invited to participate in the holiday festivities, and she shared in church services, gift-giving celebrations, a modern turkey dinner, and traditional Eskimo ice cream.

When the mail plane arrived on December 27, Ann Schell had to pack up quickly to make the flight. Only one knitter had actually begun a lace scarf, but many were excited about finishing the lessons and starting scarves on their own. Schell left additional knitting kits with instructions, yarn, and needles so other women who might become interested in the knitting project could get started and send their samples in by mail. The women who completed the workshop would act as tutors to any new knitters.

As other villages became interested and Ann Lillian Schell and Helen Howard taught workshops around the state, it was soon obvious that the project was going to be a success. Oomingmak Musk Ox Producers' Co-operative was incorporated in 1970.

One of the most luxurious and expensive fibers in the world, qiviut has been called "the golden fleece of the Arctic."

Qiviut is naturally a warm, light brown or taupe color. It can be dyed in jewel tones, and comes in weights that range from extra fine to sport-weight. A little goes a long way, in both knitting pleasure and warmth.

Photo courtesy of Folknits.

Chapter 6

Qiviut—and other lace yarns

While qiviut is an exquisite lace-knitting fiber, delightful projects can be completed in many other appropriate yarns.

One of the delights of pursuing my obsession was that I got to buy and knit with an array of qiviut yarn. I purchased some by mail order from Canada; discovered yarns and fiber in yarn stores, museum gift shops, and novelty stores all over Alaska; and got samples from several farms and yarn shops around the United States. I still can't stop touching the yarn and rubbing the scarves on my face, admiring the softness of the yarn.

Qiviut is said to be softer than cashmere, eight times warmer than sheep's wool, and the strongest of all exotic fibers. The softness and warmth are obvious, but it's hard to imagine that such sumptuous and fine yarn can be strong. When I blocked the delicate scarves I'd made, I was afraid I might tear the yarn as I stretched it to open the lace stitches. But even when I pulled a scarf several inches in both length and width, the yarn stretched beautifully without any damage.

Because down evolved as a protection against harsh environments, qiviut shares properties with fibers from other species around the world. Like down from camels, yaks, vicuñas, and cashmere goats, qiviut is lightweight, warm, and soft, but not particularly lustrous. Like all of these other fibers and like human hair, qiviut fibers are composed of three layers: cuticle, cortex, and medulla. The cuticle is the outer layer of scales. On qiviut, as on cashmere and vicuña, because the fine scales are smooth, the fiber will not felt. (Wool and mohair, with coarser, jagged

Dominic Cotignola

Qiviut is the underdown grown by musk oxen and provides the animals with warmth. Musk oxen also grow a coarse coat of guard hair, which protects them from the weather. Mixed, as shown here, the fibers don't look promising.

How do you spell "qiviut"?

The word *qiviut* is from the Inupiat word for down. Similarly to the word down in English, qiviut may refer to the soft undercoat of hair that animals grow during the winter, or to the fluffy feathers on a bird. Because Inupiat was originally a spoken, not written, language and the sounds do not correspond directly to the Roman alphabet, the word is spelled in different ways, including *qiviut, qiviuk, qiveut,* and *qiviuq.* According to the *Iñupiat Eskimo Dictionary,* the spelling of the word may differentiate between the original dual meaning and today's commercial usage:

- *qiviuq:* down (of water fowl), wool (of musk ox)
- *qiviut:* down, musk oxen wool

The term *qiviut* is used by Oomingmak Musk Ox Producers' Co-operative. The term is trademarked in Alaska to signify only products made from the underwool of the musk ox that are designed, knitted, and sold by the co-op.

scales, felt quite easily.) The cortex is the part of the fiber that determines crimp, or waviness. The medulla is the core of the fiber containing the keratin pigment that gives qiviut its unique color.

What makes qiviut so soft and caressable? It is so fine that the individual hairs are almost transparent and I can hardly see the single hairs without using a magnifying glass. Wool fibers are measured in microns. One micron is equal to 39 millionths of an inch (.000039 inch or .0009906 mm). A medium-grade wool might measure between 25 and 30 microns in diameter. A fine Merino might be between 18 and 24 microns. Very coarse wools may measure in the vicinity of 35 to 40 microns or more. Early tests on small samples of qiviut taken from captive animals found fiber diameters ranging from 11 to 17 microns, with an average staple length of 3 inches (7.6 cm). In 2001 researchers studied samples sheared from the hides of wild Canadian musk oxen and the qiviut fibers measured 16 to 20 microns with an average 2.5-inch (6.3-cm) staple length. Results of these studies put qiviut in the same category as cashmere.

However, qiviut is lighter and fluffier than cashmere. When I washed and blocked my qiviut knitting the yarn bloomed and developed a halo with a delicate, airy drape matched by no other fiber.

From fiber to yarn

Creating fine yarn from downy fiber is a tedious, labor-intensive process. In Alaska, on the Musk Ox Farm, at LARS, and in other private herds, experienced handlers comb the animals every spring when the qiviut sheds naturally. On Nunivak Island and in other areas where wild musk oxen roam, handspinners pick up tufts of qiviut found blowing in the wind or hanging on branches and fences. This is not a practical way to harvest large amounts of qiviut for commercial processing, because only small amounts are found floating around the tundra, and the fiber quickly loses its soft, luxurious hand when the sun bleaches the fragile fibers.

In Canada, where 125,000 musk oxen roam the tundra, annual hunting quotas in the Northwest Territories and Nunavut allow Inuit hunters to harvest musk oxen for meat.

The hides are preserved and later sheared. In 2004 Inuit hunters harvested almost 800 animals from Banks Island to sell through Jacques Cartier Clothier and at the Inuvialuit Development Corporation office in Inuvik. The Kitikmeot Hunters and Trappers

Association of Nunavut has a joint project with Mini-Mills Ltd., the manufacturer of fiber-processing equipment based on Prince Edward Island, to market qiviut fiber and products.

After it is harvested, the mass of raw fiber begins its journey to becoming luxury yarn. Because of the variable quality of fiber from different parts of the body, sorters separate each fleece into sections according to fiber quality and length. (At LARS, qiviut from the shoulders is often saved for handspinners, who require the highest quality fiber.) If the fibers are particularly dirty, they are sometimes scoured, or washed. Finally, the fiber is dehaired to remove the guard hairs, so only the soft down remains for spinning. Because the long outer coat does not shed, only a few guard hairs come out as the qiviut is combed. Qiviut does contain some "medium" fibers that may measure up to 50 microns in diameter. These fibers are soft and fine near the roots but thicker and coarser near the tips, and they tend to shed with the qiviut. Fiber sheared from the hides of animals taken in hunts is full of guard hair and must be processed thoroughly to ensure a high-quality finished yarn.

Buying qiviut yarn

To make sure you have a wonderful experience knitting with qiviut and end up with a garment that you will treasure, take the time to select your yarn carefully:

- Consider both mill-spun and handspun yarns. Mill-spun yarns are available in large quantities from commercial processors. Handspun yarns may be more difficult to find, but they are unique and often preserve the characteristics of the raw fiber in a way that is not possible in mechanized processing.
- If possible, feel the yarn before you buy it. If you order by mail, be sure to check the return policy in case you are not satisfied with the product you receive.
- Buy one skein for swatching first. Why lay out a large sum of cash before you've tested the yarn and pattern and are certain you want to proceed?

At the Musk Ox Farm, familiar handlers gently remove qiviut without damaging it or hurting the animals. Here Wendy is combing out down.

Photo by Bill Bacon courtesy of Oomingmak Musk Ox Producers' Co-operative.

- Balance quality against cost. Some less-expensive yarns may have guard hair. Do you have the patience to pick it out?
- Soft yarns made from short-staple fibers sometimes pill. Although qiviut seems less susceptible to pilling than merino or other fine fibers, it does form a fluffy halo that can pill if treated harshly. Will this bother you? If so, consider substituting another lace-weight yarn in your pattern (see pages 87–89 for suggestions).

Qiviut is suitable for a variety of projects. Because it is much warmer than other luxury fibers or wool, qiviut is perfectly suited for knitting lightweight, lofty fabrics that trap air and have properties similar to polar fleece. Unlike wool, qiviut is not very springy. If you are designing your own qiviut garments or accessories,

Qiviut: Spinning it

In the early days of the Oomingmak Co-op, test projects were completed with both handspun and mill-spun yarn. As a result, mill-spun yarn was chosen for the production of commercial products (in part because it was more appealing to men, although no reasons were specified). The handspun yarn for testing was beautiful and unusual. I saw the sample swatches that are still stored in the co-op's library. Singles made of 100 percent qiviut were knitted into a fabric similar to the lace products made from mill-spun lace-weight yarn. Samples of qiviut carded with silk, as well as a strand of qiviut plied with silk, had unusual textures. The soft qiviut plied with the lustrous silk is unlike any other yarn I have seen.

Today, raw qiviut fiber and prepared roving are available in limited quantities. If you purchase raw fiber, you will have to manually pluck the guard hairs from the qiviut and remove any other debris, such as skin flakes or plant matter. In most cases, qiviut requires no other cleaning or preparation,

although it can be lightly carded with hand cards or on a drum carder with fine (fur) carding cloth.

Because qiviut is so warm, consider blending it with wool, silk, or other natural fibers if you want a heavier yarn or if you are knitting a garment that will benefit from elasticity in the yarn. Blending other fibers with qiviut also cuts down on the cost.

Guard hair can also be spun—alone or blended with a long-staple wool—into a strong, lustrous yarn perfect for making rugs and blankets or sturdy outerwear garments.

Dianne Nash, of Windy Valley Muskox, spinning qiviut.

Photo © John Nash. Used by permission.

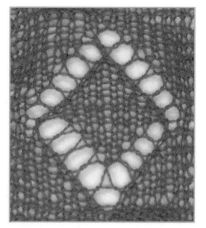

Merino

Alpaca

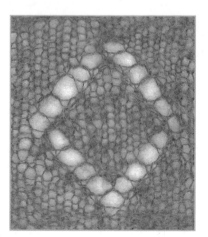

Mohair

consider using garter stitch or seed stitch instead of ribbing. Ribbing works best when worked in a yarn elastic enough to let it pull in slightly; the other stitches form borders that perform well without elasticity. (See Chapter 9 for several options and charts.)

Qiviut yarn can be found in weights ranging from extra-fine lace-weight to sport-weight. The fiber is most often spun in fine weights because it is so warm and so expensive. Fingering- and lace-weight yarns are easiest to find. The yarn blooms when washed, creating a wonderful halo and filling in the spaces between stitches, so qiviut can be knitted at a looser gauge than other fine yarns.

In addition to natural taupe, qiviut yarn is available in many beautiful colors.

Other lace yarns

Because qiviut is rare and expensive, you may want to knit some of the projects in this book using other fibers. Many excellent yarns in a variety of fibers are appropriate for substitution.

Protein, or animal-source, fibers make warm, breathable yarns that are easy to knit because the fibers have natural give, or stretch. Depending on the type of animal and specific breed, yarns from animal fibers can be soft enough to place next to a baby's skin or strong enough to wipe your feet on.

- **Wool** is the most common animal fiber and comes from the fleece of sheep. Wool is warm and breathable and can absorb up to 30 percent of its weight in water without feeling wet. Merino wool is quite soft and has a gentle drape after blocking. It works well in lace projects. See page 4 for a photo showing the North Star Tam (from page 126) knitted in both lace-weight qiviut and fingering-weight wool.
- **Alpaca and llama** fibers are spun into yarns that are similar to wool but have less elasticity and a beautiful drape. These yarns can be very soft, but they are usually denser and weigh more than wool yarns of the same thickness.
- **Mohair and cashmere** yarns are made from the fleece of goats. Cashmere is spun from the down, or undercoat, of the cashmere goat; mohair is spun from the fleece of the Angora goat. Cashmere is incredibly soft, but slightly denser than qiviut, and it does not bloom as much after washing. Lace-weight

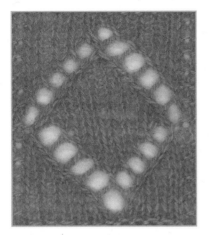

Cashmere

Camel

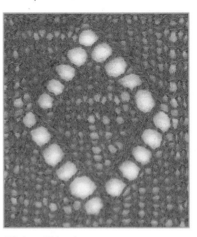

Silk/wool blend

Cotton (mercerized)

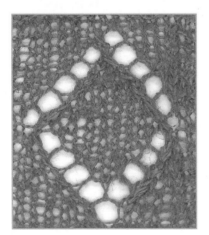

Linen

mohair knits into a light, fluffy fabric that has a halo similar to the bloom that qiviut develops after several washings.

- **Camel and yak** are similar to cashmere and are available in lovely natural shades of tan and brown.
- **Silk** is the only common protein fiber that does not come from the fleece of an animal. Silk comes from the fibers that form the cocoon of the *Bombyx mori* moth. The silkworm, or caterpillar, spins a very strong fiber that can be made into yarn or fabric that is cool in summer and warm in winter. Because it has little elasticity, silk drapes beautifully when knitted into fine lace patterns.

Cellulose, or plant-source, fibers usually have less elasticity than protein fibers and often make stronger yarns. Some are even used to make ropes.

- **Cotton** is a versatile fiber, grown by plant species of the genus *Gossypium*, that can be spun into a strong and absorbent yarn. Mercerized cotton is lustrous and drapes well, while unmercerized cotton is more absorbent and softer. (Mercerization is a chemical treatment.) Fabrics made from cotton tend to stretch out of shape as they get older. For scarves and shawls, this is not terribly important. Fitted items, however, may lose their shapes after several washings.
- **Linen**, made from flax, is the oldest known natural fiber. Linen does not absorb water well and it wrinkles easily. Because of this, it is often blended with other fibers for use in garments.

Hemp

- **Hemp** comes from a plant in the nettle family that can be raised with no herbicides or pesticides. The resulting eco-friendly yarn can be almost identical to linen. Hemp is often blended with cotton or wool to create a softer yarn.

Man-made fibers are not appropriate for fine lace knitting. Acrylic and other man-made fibers snap back to their original shapes after washing and drying. They will not hold their shapes after blocking. In knitting, yarn-overs and other patterns disappear in a blur.

Yarns can also be blends or combinations of fibers. Blends may be combinations of two or more natural fibers, or combinations of natural and synthetic fibers. For example, mohair yarn may be spun with a nylon core to hold the fluffy mohair fibers together. For vests or sweaters, qiviut blended with wool or wool and silk makes incredibly soft yet durable garments.

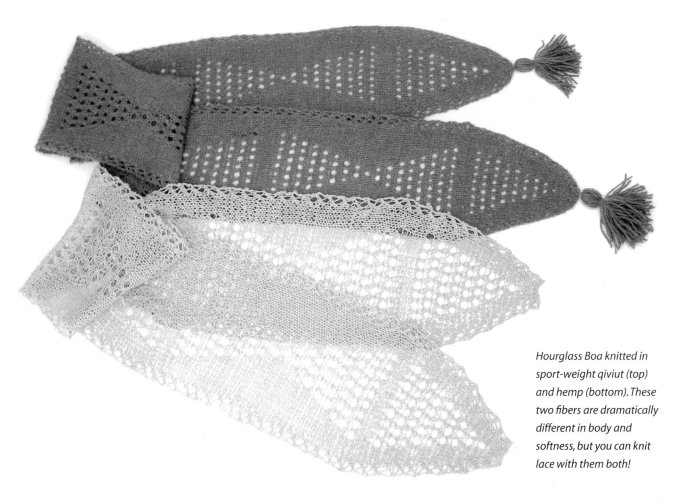

Hourglass Boa knitted in sport-weight qiviut (top) and hemp (bottom). These two fibers are dramatically different in body and softness, but you can knit lace with them both!

89

I thought I would never be able to knit lace—until I stumbled onto Dorothy Reade's simple techniques, which gave the Oomingmak Co-op knitters such a firm foundation in the craft.

Chapter 7

Lace-knitting workshop

Tip for experienced lace knitters:
Look through the introductory material explaining the techniques that the co-op knitters use, some of which are unique. When you come to the swatches, skip swatch 1 and work swatches 2 and 3 using the chart from the project you want to knit.

Photo opposite by Dominic Cotignola.

*I*f you have not yet worked with lace, this chapter will give you all the information you need to approach this type of knitting with confidence. If I was able to learn how to knit lace using these techniques, I know you can, too!

For years I tried to learn how to knit lace and was frustrated as I failed each time. I finally gave up because I wanted to have fun knitting and enjoy my hobby. I was able to knit cables, Fair Isle, intarsia, and even entrelac with no problems, but lace stymied me. I thought I would never be able to knit lace—until I stumbled onto Dorothy Reade's simple techniques, which gave the Oomingmak Co-op knitters such a firm foundation in the craft.

Today, most lace-knitting patterns are charted. As it turns out, this was one of the keys to success for me. In my early attempts to knit lace, I tried to work from patterns with line-by-line instructions and no charts. Translating from the words on the page to the stitches on the needles proved all but impossible for me. I put a sticky note on my instructions, put markers between repeats, and counted stitches after each row. Still, by the third or fourth row I had made a mistake and was faced with the daunting challenge of ripping back my knitting. With lace, ripping and then continuing the work is often difficult. I ended up starting over again and again, until I gave up.

When I discovered lace charts, I was well on my way to success. (For instructions on reading lace charts, see pages 95–97.)

The second key to my eventual success with knitting lace was Dorothy Reade's decrease technique. Lace knitting "draws" a design by using yarn-overs to create holes in the fabric. Every time you create one of these holes you must make a corresponding decrease. Otherwise you will just keep adding stitches (one for every yarn-over) and the so the knitting will get wider . . . and wider. . . .

1 & 2 Qiviut/merino/silk blend; cobweb lace-weight and fingering-weight.
3 Qiviut/merino blend, lace-weight.
4 & 5 Pure qiviut, fingering-weight and sport-weight.

Photo courtesy of Caryll Designs.

The decreases also draw lines that outline the design. A simple *knit-two-together (k2tog)* decrease is used to draw a line that slants to the right. Drawing a line that slants to the left turns out to be a little more complicated.

In traditional lace patterns, the left-slanting decrease is *slip 1, knit 1, pass the slipped stitch over (slip 1, k1, psso or skp)*. Contemporary designs more frequently use the *slip, slip, knit (ssk)* decrease. Both of these decreases disrupt the rhythm of your knitting with extra movements. You are creating one decrease stitch, but with three motions. In her patterns, Dorothy Reade's left-slanting decrease is *knit two together through the back loops (k2tog-tbl)*, thus allowing you to maintain the rhythm: one motion produces one stitch. (For instructions on this decrease, see page 104.)

The final key to my success was discovering the three-step lace-knitting tutorial that Ann Lillian Schell used to teach workshops to the co-op's first knitters. In this process, you first knit a simple swatch in worsted-weight yarn on 3.75 mm (size 5 U.S.) knitting needles. After you learn the basic lace stitches, you move to 3.25 mm (size 3 U.S.) needles and fingering-weight yarn and work a swatch with smaller stitches. Finally, when you feel comfortable with the lace stitches, you do a third swatch with the needles and yarn specified in your project—and by this point you're ready for lace-weight yarn. Practicing on the heavier wool yarn and larger needles gave me the confidence to learn the lace-knitting techniques before I had to fumble with tiny needles and thread-like lace yarn. (For my version of Ann Lillian Schell's three-step lace-knitting tutorial, see page 111–114.)

The following sections cover everything you need to know in order to practice and then to embark on your own lace-knitting project.

Tools

Knitting needles come in many shapes, sizes, and materials. Each set of needles behaves differently. Take the time to try different kinds and see what's most comfortable for you.

Circular, straight, or double-pointed needles?

For lace knitting, I like straight needles 8 to 10 inches (20 to 25 cm) long best. With the fine yarn used for knitting lace, you can easily fit a large number of stitches on short needles. For narrow projects, such as scarves, it can be nice to have even shorter needles. Here's where double-pointed needles come in handy: use just two from the set and put a point protector on one end of each needle to keep the stitches from sliding off.

Even the best quality circular needles, with smooth joins between the cable and the needle, can be cumbersome for knitting lace. Unless your tension is unusually relaxed, it can be difficult to slide the stitches from the thin cable back onto the needle. If the join between the cable and the needle has a bump, knitting lace can become virtually impossible. Pulling and tugging to move the stitches around the cable may distort your gauge and stretch the yarn-overs out of shape. I only use circular needles for lace projects that are knitted in the round.

What size of needles?

Lace can be made with any size knitting needles and many different types of yarn. The projects in this book are all knitted with thin yarns varying from threadlike extra-fine lace-weight to heavier, but still thin, sport-weight. For these projects, I used relatively small needles.

All of the co-op knitters use 3.25 mm (size 3 U.S.) needles to knit a test swatch. Then they go up or down in needle size from 1.75 mm (size 00 U.S.) to 3.75 mm (size 5 U.S.) to get a gauge within the tolerances of Oomingmak products. Even with that, there are variations in the finished knitting. When the projects are washed and blocked at the co-op store in Anchorage, the items are sorted and tagged by size. Items received from loose knitters are marked "large," and items from tight knitters are marked "small." For the scarves and shawls in this book, exact gauge is not critical. However, for fitted items such as the fingerless gloves on page 150 and the hat on page 122, reproducing the specified gauge is important for getting the correct fit. I introduce the technique of changing gauge to get different sizes in the Grass-Basket Cropped Ruana Vest on page 146.

Metal, bamboo, wood, or plastic needles?

For beginning lace knitters, plastic or bamboo needles are good choices. They are warm and smooth and not as slippery as nickel-plated metal needles. Wooden needles are also comfortable, but I can't use wooden needles smaller than 3.25 mm (size 3 U.S.) without breaking them. Bamboo holds up much better for me

Lace-knitting needle sizes

Metric (mm)	U.S.
1.75	00
2	0
2.25	1
2.75	2
3.25	3
3.5	4
3.75	5
4	6
4.5	7

under stress than wood does. Some painted aluminum needles have enough texture to keep your knitting securely on the needle, but nickel-plated needles are very slick. Expert knitters can use nickel-plated needles for lace, but avoid them for lace unless you know what you are doing; you are likely to drop stitches and get frustrated.

Dorothy Reade said that knitting needles made from different materials change the texture of knitting. Modern needles provide many choices, and I've updated her suggestions with my own observations.

➹ Plastic needles result in a flowing fabric with a soft texture and drape. Different brands have differently shaped points. Narrow points make it easier to work decreases.

➹ Wooden and bamboo needles give a medium texture and are lightweight and comfortable to work with.

➹ According to Dorothy Reade, metal needles give the tightest, firmest texture. She may have been talking about the painted aluminum needles available at craft and hobby stores. Nickel-plated needles were not yet available. I've found that nickel-plated needles give a very loose texture, and many knitters need to go down one or two sizes to get the correct gauge on these needles.

➹ Dorothy Reade claimed that circular needles give a medium texture, slightly different from the texture obtained using straight needles of the same material. She warned against switching between straight and circular needles in the same project. I have found no difference between straight and circular needles of the same material.

For beginning lace knitters, plastic or bamboo needles are good choices. They are warm and smooth and not too slippery.

Symbol systems

Dorothy Reade	This book	
X	☐	knit (on right side)
✓	—	purl (on right side)
B	Ⴘ	knit through back loop (ktbl)
●	O	yarn over
∧	∧	slip 1, k2tog, psso
╱	╱	k2tog
╲	╲	k2tog through back loops (k2tog-tbl)
2	∨	increase 1 (or make-one increase)

Reading lace charts

Today, we may take easy-to-follow charts for granted, but before Dorothy Reade's book, *25 Original Knitting Designs,* was published in 1965, knitters were stuck with deciphering long, error-prone, written instructions that were less than enlightening. Line-by-line instructions are still common in some books, and not all knitters are familiar with charts. The following pages take you step-by-step through the process of reading and knitting from charts.

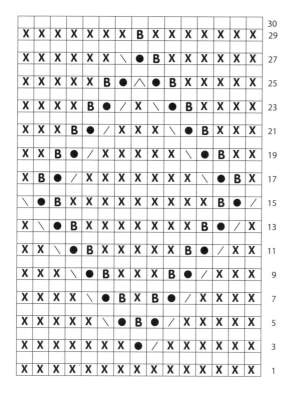

The lace charts in this book use modern symbols that I find easier to read than those in Dorothy Reade's early charts. The keys to the two symbol systems are on the previous page. Dorothy Reade charted all rows. I chart only the rows where patterning occurs.

Above left is a pattern chart using the symbols from Dorothy Reade's 25 Original Knitting Designs. *Below left is the same pattern as I chart it. The box shows how the same chart is written in line-by-line instructions.*

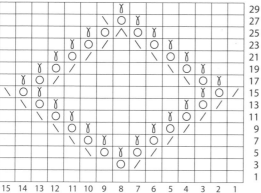

Line-by-line instructions corresponding to charts

Row 1: Knit.

Row 2 and all wrong-side rows: Purl.

Row 3: K6, k2tog, yo, k7.

Row 5: K5, k2tog, yo, ktbl, yo, k2tog tbl, k5.

Row 7: K4, k2tog, yo, ktbl, k1, ktbl, yo, k2tog tbl, k4.

Row 9: K3, k2tog, yo, ktbl, k3, ktbl, yo, k2tog tbl, k3.

Row 11: K2, k2tog, yo, ktbl, k5, ktbl, yo, k2tog tbl, k2.

Row 13: K1, k2tog, yo, ktbl, k7, ktbl, yo, k2tog tbl, k1.

Row 15: K2tog, yo, ktbl, k9, ktbl, yo, k2tog tbl.

Row 17: K1, ktbl, yo, k2tog tbl, k7, k2tog, yo, ktbl, k1.

Row 19: K2, ktbl, yo, k2tog tbl, k5, k2tog, yo, ktbl, k2.

Row 21: K3, ktbl, yo, k2tog tbl, k3, k2tog, yo, ktbl, k3.

Row 23: K4, ktbl, yo, k2tog tbl, k1, k2tog, yo, ktbl, k4.

Row 25: K5, ktbl, yo, sl1, k2tog, psso, yo, ktbl, k5.

Row 27: K6, ktbl, yo, k2tog tbl, k6.

Row 29: K7, ktbl, k7.

Basic instructions

Each square on the chart represents one stitch. The symbol in the square tells you what to do when you get to that stitch in the row.

Each row of the chart represents one row of knitting. The bottom of the chart is the first row. As you knit, you move up the chart one row at a time.

Circular knitting

In circular knitting, you work in the round, and the right side (RS) of the knitting is always facing you. Read all chart rows from right to left. For example, row 11 of this chart reads: k2, k2tog, yo, ktbl, k5, ktbl, yo, k2tog-tbl, k2. (*Knit 2, knit 2 together, yarn-over, knit through the back loop, knit 5, knit through the back loop, yarn-over, knit 2 together through the back loops, knit 2.*)

Flat knitting

In flat knitting, you work back and forth, turning your work at the end of each row. The first row is worked with the right side of the knitting facing you; the second row is worked with the wrong side facing.

On many lace charts, only half of the rows are shown. You can see that this is the case on the sample chart because the rows are numbered 1, 3, 5, and so on.

If only right-side rows are shown on the chart, what about the even-numbered, or wrong-side, rows? You either knit or purl all the way across each wrong-side row. This will usually be stated in the directions. Knitting all the way across each wrong-side row produces a garter-stitch background. Purling all the way across produces a stockinette background.

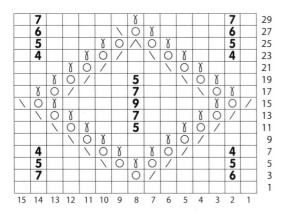

This chart shows numbered rows (along the right edge) and stitches (along the bottom). Only the right-side rows are shown. On flat knitting, wrong-side (even-numbered) rows will be knitted (for a garter-stitch background) or purled (for a stockinette-stitch background). On circular knitting, even-numbered rows are still right-side rows. They will be purled for garter-stitch or knitted for stockinette-stitch.

Bold numbers within the chart make it easier to count plain knit stitches when there are a lot of them in a row.

If wrong-side rows are shown on the chart,

- Odd rows are the right side of the work. Read these rows from right to left.
- Even rows are the wrong side of the work. Read these rows from left to right.

This chart for flat knitting shows both right-side (odd-numbered) and wrong-side (even-numbered) rows.

The odd-numbered rows are worked right to left (numbers along right edge). The even-numbered rows are worked left to right (numbers along left edge).

To work in circular knitting, read all rows from right to left.

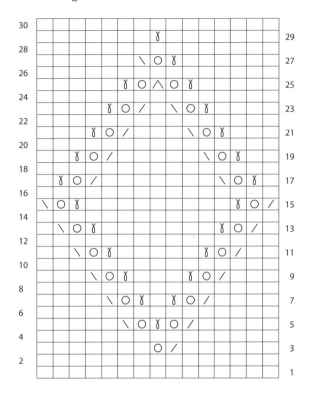

In flat knitting, you may also find extra stitches at the beginning and end of each row. These stitches center the pattern and result in clean edges on the left and right. (These balancing stitches are not necessary for circular knitting because there are no edges.)

The stitches marked with asterisks are used in flat knitting to center the pattern. They are not required in circular knitting.

The basic repeat unit of this pattern is shaded.

Pattern repeats

To produce a given pattern, you may need to repeat either groups of stitches (across a row) or sequences of rows—or both. For large items, you will most often work a specified group of stitches more than once as you move across the row. Each group of stitches like this is called a *repeat*. You may also repeat a series of rows in the chart several times one after the other. The repeat is indicated by a shading.

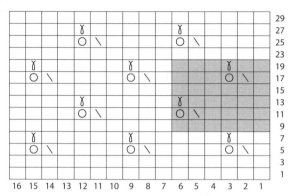

Techniques

Lace knitting uses the same basic techniques and stitches as other styles of knitting. However, there are many ways to knit, purl, increase, and decrease, and not all are appropriate for lace. In addition, because lace is very stretchy, you'll need to use loose cast-on and bind-off techniques. Otherwise, the edges of your knitting will draw in or you'll end up with a stiff edge on a pliable fabric.

The following sections explain Dorothy Reade's techniques, which I have used, with a few modifications, for all the projects in this book.

Abbreviations

dp	double-pointed
k	knit
k2tog	knit 2 stitches together
m1	make-one increase
p	purl
pm	place a marker
psso	pass slipped stitch over
RS	right-side, right side
sl	slip
sm	slip the marker
st	stitch
sts	stitches
tbl	through back loop (twists stitch)
WS	wrong-side, wrong side
yo	yarn-over

Casting on (abbreviated CO)

Long-tail cast-on

The long-tail cast-on creates an elastic edge appropriate for most lace projects. Cast on loosely, or over two needles held together, to create a stretchy edge that will have the same flexibility as the openwork lace stitches.

1 To get started, pull out a "long tail" of yarn. Make a slipknot and put it on the needle. This is the first stitch.

2 With the tail of the yarn over your left thumb and the yarn attached to the ball over your index finger, pull the strands open. Grasp the strands in your left palm, and pull the needle down to form a V with the yarn.

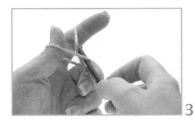

3a With your right hand, insert the needle into the loop on your thumb, from bottom to top.

3b Bring the needle around the yarn on your index finger from right to left, catch the yarn, and pull it back down through the loop on your thumb.

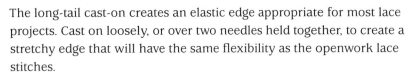

4 Pull your thumb out of the loop. You now have another stitch on the needle. Reposition your thumb under the tail, and tug gently to tighten the new stitch. Don't release the strands held in your palm.

5 Repeat steps 3 and 4 until you have the required number of stitches on the right needle.

Tip: *For the long tail, measure approximately 1 inch (2.5 cm) of yarn for every stitch you want to cast on. From your nose to the tips of your fingers is about 1 yard of yarn and will produce about 36 stitches.*

Cable cast-on

The cable cast-on creates a stable, decorative edge. Although it is not stretchy like the long-tail cast-on, this technique creates a firm edge that helps qiviut keep its shape on fitted items like the Wrist Warmers on page 122 and the Grass-Basket Cropped Ruana Vest on page 146. Dorothy Reade also recommended the cable cast-on for socks and for sleeve beginnings.

1 Make a slipknot about 4 inches (10 cm) from the end of the yarn. This is the first stitch.

2 Knit one stitch. Leave the slipknot on the left needle, and place the new stitch on the left needle as well. You now have two stitches on the *left* needle and the right needle is empty.

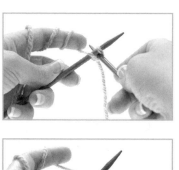

3 Insert the right needle *between* the last two stitches on the left needle and wrap the yarn as if to knit.

4 Pull the yarn through.

5 Place the new stitch on the left needle as shown.

6 Repeat steps 3 through 5 for the required number of stitches.

Tip: *Don't tighten the new stitch until after you insert the needle between the two stitches.*

The basic lace stitches

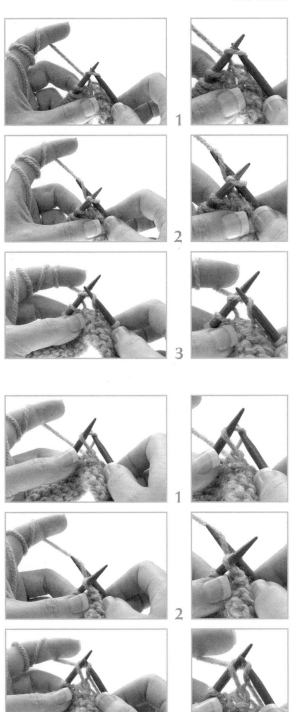

Knit (abbreviated k)

The knit stitch is one of the two main stitches in knitting. A regular knit stitch creates a V on the surface of the knitting and a bump on the back of the work.

1 With the working yarn in *back* of the left needle, insert the right needle under the left needle and into the first stitch from *front to back*.

2 Wrap the working yarn around the right needle counterclockwise.

3 Pull the yarn through the loop on the left needle.

4 Drop the old stitch from the left needle. You now have one new knit stitch on the right needle.

Knit through back loop (abbreviated ktbl)

This variation of the knit stitch twists the new stitch and creates an X on the surface of the knitting. It is used to emphasize lace patterns by creating a crisp outline.

1 With the working yarn in *back* of the left needle, insert the right needle under the left needle and into the *back loop* of the first stitch.

2 Wrap the working yarn around the right needle counterclockwise.

3 Pull the yarn through the loop on the left needle.

4 Drop the old stitch from the left needle. You now have one new twisted stitch on the right needle.

Purl (abbreviated p) ⬚

The purl stitch is the second main stitch in knitting. It is essentially the reverse of a knit stitch; a knit stitch worked on the wrong side of the work produces a purl on the front side. The purl stitch creates a bump on the front and a V on the back.

1 With the working yarn in *front* of the left needle, insert the right needle into the first stitch *from back to front*.

2 Wrap the working yarn around the right needle counterclockwise.

3 Pull the yarn through.

4 Drop the old stitch from the left needle. You now have one new purl stitch on the right needle.

1a

1b

Yarn-over (abbreviated yo) ⬚

A yarn-over creates a small hole in your knitting and adds one stitch.

1 Bring the yarn between the needles to the front, and then over the needle again to the back of the work to begin the next knit stitch.

1a: Yarn to the front of the needle, over it, and to back.

1b: Working the first stitch after the yarn-over.

2 On the next row, work the yarn-over as a regular knit or purl stitch.

1

2a

2b

Double yarn-over (abbreviated yo 2x) ⬚⬚

A double yarn-over creates a large hole in your knitting and adds two stitches.

1 Bring the yarn between the needles to the front, over the needle again to the back of the work, then repeat. You should have two wraps of yarn around the right needle before you make the next knit stitch.

2 On the next row, when you come to the double yarn-over, purl in the first loop (2a) and knit in the second (2b).

Double yarn-over completed on following row

Knit two together (abbreviated k2tog)

Knit two together is a *right-slanting* decrease that removes one stitch from your knitting. This is one way to compensate for adding a stitch with a yarn-over.

~ Insert the needle through the first *two loops* on the left needle at the same time, and work them together as a regular knit stitch.

Knit two together through the back loops (abbreviated k2tog-tbl)

Knit two together through the back loops is a *left-slanting* decrease that removes one stitch from your knitting.

~ Insert the needle *through the back loops of the first two stitches* on the left needle at once, and work them together as a knit stitch.

Note: *Dorothy Reade says that k2tog-tbl is the true opposite of k2tog, but I disagree. The slip, slip, knit (ssk) decrease is technically more a mirror of k2tog, but the difference in appearance in the final product is negligible. I find that ssk disrupts my knitting rhythm and makes it more difficult for me to memorize the lace charts; however, if you are comfortable with the ssk decrease, feel free to substitute it wherever k2tog-tbl is specified.*

Slip one (abbreviated slip1)

Slipping a stitch moves it from the left needle to the right needle without creating a new knit or purl stitch.

1 Insert the right needle through the next stitch on the left needle as if you were going to knit the stitch (called "as if to knit").

2 Slip the stitch onto the right needle.

Slip one, knit two together, pass slipped stitch over
(slip 1, k2tog, psso)

This *double-decrease* removes two stitches from your knitting at one time.

1 & 2 Same as for *slip 1* on previous page.

3 K2tog: Knit two stitches together (see k2tog on the previous page).

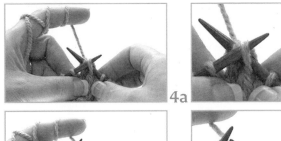

4 Psso: Insert the left needle into the slipped stitch on the right needle (4a), draw it over the knitted stitch (4b), then drop it off the needles.

Increasing

Knit into front and back of stitch

To increase without adding a hole to the knitting with a yarn-over, simply knit into the front loop and then into the back loop of the same stitch. This is the only increase method Dorothy Reade used in her knitting. If you have another favorite technique, feel free to substitute.

Make 1 (abbreviated M1)

Knitting into the front and back of the stitch makes a small bump on the fabric. Sometimes this doesn't show on fine lacework, but I use the *make-one (M1) increase* because it adds one stitch invisibly.

1 With the tip of the left needle, lift the strand between the last stitch worked and the next stitch on the needle. Place the strand onto the left needle.

2 Knit into the *back* of the newly created loop to "make one" stitch.

Binding off (abbreviated BO)

Basic bind-off

This bind-off is worked as a regular row, with each stitch eliminated after it is worked. Many knitters have trouble binding off loosely. If you have this problem, first try binding off using a needle several sizes larger than the needle used for your knitting. If your bind-off is still tight, try the stretchy bind-off below.

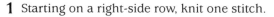

1 Starting on a right-side row, knit one stitch.

2 Knit another stitch. You now have two stitches on the right needle.

3 Insert the left needle into the second stitch from the tip of right needle (the one you knitted first).

4 Pass this stitch over the stitch closest to the tip of the needle (the one you knitted second), dropping it off the needles. One stitch remains on the right needle.

5 Repeat steps 2 to 4 until one stitch remains. Fasten off.

Stretchy bind-off

After searching for a bind-off technique that was easy and flexible, I found this technique in *A Treasury of Magical Knitting* by Cat Bordhi.

1 Knit two stitches. Put the two stitches back on the left needle and knit them together through the back loops (see k2tog-tbl on page 104).

2 Knit one. Put the two stitches now on the right needle back on the left needle and knit two together through the back loops (k2tog-tbl).

3 Repeat step 2 until one stitch remains. Fasten off.

Tip: *Three times the length of the join is usually barely enough. Try three-and-a-half to four times the length of the join. More is better than less, because adding new yarn in the middle of grafting is a nuisance.*

Sewing seams

Dorothy Reade suggested using a diagonal whip-stitch seam to sew pieces together. For scarves that are knitted in two halves and then joined, I use the Kitchener stitch to invisibly graft the pieces together. For the Grass-Basket Cropped Ruana Vest, I use the three-needle bind-off to join the shoulders.

Kitchener stitch (grafting)

For Kitchener stitch, you must have the same number of stitches in each group to be joined together. Break off the working yarn, leaving a strand long enough to work all the way across the join. Thread this working strand into a sewing-style yarn needle with a blunt point.

1 (Set-up) Hold the two pieces together on the two knitting needles, wrong sides together, positioned so the working strand comes from the righthand stitch on the front needle.

1a: Insert the sewing needle into the first stitch on the back needle as if to knit, but don't take the stitch off its needle.

1b: Now insert the sewing needle into the first stitch on the front needle as if to purl, and again don't take the stitch off the needle.

2 (Back needle)

2a: Take the sewing needle to the back needle and insert it in the first stitch as if to purl—now remove that stitch from its needle.

2b: Insert the sewing needle into the next stitch as if to knit but do not remove it.

3 (Front needle)

3a: Take the sewing needle to the front needle and insert it in the first stitch as if to knit—now remove that stitch from its needle.

3b: Insert the sewing needle into the next stitch as if to purl but do not remove it.

4 Repeat steps 2 and 3 until one stitch remains on each needle. Follow the established pattern as well as possible with these two stitches. One will be removed from its needle after the second pass of the sewing needle; there will be no second stitch on that needle to go through before moving to the other needle. The final stitch will only be entered once with the sewing needle. Fasten off.

Three-needle bind-off

The three-needle bind-off lets you join two pieces of knitting by binding them off together. This technique is the same as the basic bind-off, except that you are joining stitches from two pieces of knitting as you bind off.

Both pieces must have the same number of stitches. If you join the pieces with right sides together, the seam creates a straight line. If you join the pieces with wrong sides together, the seam creates a decorative ridge.

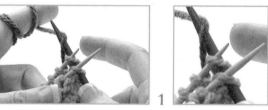

1 Holding the two pieces together on two needles, insert a third needle as if to knit into the first stitch on the front needle and also into the first stitch on the back needle. Knit these two stitches together, making one stitch.

2 Knit another stitch as in step 1. You now have two stitches on the right needle.

3 Insert the left needle into the second stitch from the tip of the right needle and pass it over the first stitch, dropping it off the needles. One stitch remains on the right needle.

4 Repeat steps 2 and 3 until one stitch remains. Fasten off.

Keeping track of your knitting

To keep track of where you are on the knitting chart, put a sticky note *above* the row you are knitting. That way, you will be able to see the rows that you have completed and can compare your knitting to the chart. The row you are knitting will be directly below the sticky note, making it almost impossible to lose your place.

To keep track of the right side and wrong side of your work, mark one needle with a colored rubber band or a spot of bright nail polish. Cast on with the other needle. The marked needle will be in your right hand whenever you are knitting an odd-numbered, right-side row. If you would like, you can fasten a safety pin to the right side after you have knitted a few rows.

To separate pattern repeats, place markers (abbreviated pm) between repeats. Make your own markers by tying a small loop near the end of a 6-inch (15-cm) piece of string in a color that will stand out against your knitting. Put the loop on the needle

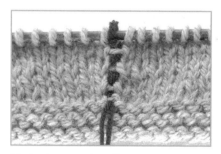
Marker to separate pattern repeats

between the repeats. Slip the marker (abbreviated sm) whenever you come to it. The tail will be trapped in the knitting, so you can clearly see the line between horizontal pattern repeats.

Fixing mistakes

At the Oomingmak Co-op store in Anchorage, staff members carefully look over every item received from knitters. If these professional knitters sometimes make mistakes and drop stitches, you probably will, too! But don't worry; minor errors are easy to fix. You don't have to wait until your piece is finished to fix mistakes. It is easiest to fix errors as soon as you notice them.

If you find that you have one too many or too few stitches, look carefully at your knitting. Does the pattern look right? Can you see a run, or ladder, in the work? If the pattern looks all right and there is no run, simply increase or decrease to the correct number of stitches and continue following the chart.

Dropped stitch

If you later find a dropped stitch, attach a safety pin or a piece of contrasting yarn to it on the wrong side of the work so you can find it later. When you finish knitting, put a 6-inch (15-cm) piece of matching yarn through the dropped stitch, and weave both ends into the surrounding background. This will secure the stitch so it will not run.

A run or ladder in an area of plain knitting

If you find a run in an area of plain knitting, use a crochet hook to "re-knit" the dropped stitch up the ladder.

1 Insert a crochet hook from front to back through the loop at the bottom of the ladder.

2 Draw the lowest ladder rung through the loop of the dropped stitch and to the front of the work. This will create a new loop and raise the bottom of the ladder one row.

Repeat steps 1 and 2 until you reach the current row of knitting. Place the recovered stitch onto the knitting needle.

A run or ladder in a section of garter stitch

If the dropped stitch is in a section of garter stitch, you will need to re-insert your crochet hook to pull up each new row because the direction in which the loop pulls through alternates from row to row. Be sure to pull through each loop from the next available strand, working your way up in sequence. Because garter stitch is the same on both sides, you can work with either side facing you. For this process, the side toward you will be called the front and the side away from you will be called the back. Unless otherwise instructed, keep the laddered strands on the back of the work.

- To pull up a *knit loop*, insert the crochet hook from *front to back* through the open loop. Pull up the bottom-most strand from behind the work and through the loop on the hook. The strand will be pulled toward the front of the work.
- To pull up a *purl loop*, move the next available (bottom-most) strand to the front of the work. Insert the crochet hook from *back to front* through the open loop. Pull the repositioned strand through the loop on the hook. The strand will be pulled toward the back of the work.

A run or ladder in a section of lace patterning

If you find a run in the middle of lace patterning, if you drop several stitches, or if your pattern does not look right and you can't find the mistake, you may have to take out a few rows of knitting. This can be arduous in lace knitting. Because the yarn is fine and often softly spun, it is better to "un-knit" one stitch at a time, rather than simply remove your needles and tear out the work.

Working slowly and carefully, un-knit backward until you come to an even-numbered row just below the area that has the mistake. (In this book, all even-numbered rows are knitted or purled, so there are no yarn-overs on these rows.) Locate where you are on the chart, and continue knitting from this point.

Missed yarn-over

If you notice that you have forgotten to make a yarn-over on the previous row, simply lift the bar between the two stitches where the yarn-over belongs onto the left needle. Then knit or purl this added yarn-over as you normally would.

Lace knitting 1–2–3

This teaching method was used by Ann Lillian Schell and Helen Howard at the early workshops for the Oomingmak Co-op. I have adapted the method and added new charts to prepare you for knitting the projects in this book. You will knit three swatches, using progressively smaller yarn and needles. The first swatch is a simple introduction to the stitches and techniques. The second and third swatches are more complex. If you are experienced with lace, skip swatch 1 and work swatches 2 and 3 with the pattern of your choice.

Swatch number	1	2	3
Needles	4.5 mm (size 7 U.S.)	3.75 mm (size 5 U.S.)	3.25 mm (size 3 U.S.)
Yarn	worsted-weight	fingering-weight	lace-weight

Measuring gauge

Stitch gauge is important in almost all knitting projects. If the stitch gauge is not exact, your garment will not be the size indicated in the pattern. On knitted lace, gauge is measured *after blocking*. On some projects, this will be only slightly different from the gauge before blocking, but on others the difference may be drastic.

For shawls and scarves, gauge is less critical than for fitted items such as vests and gloves. Row gauge is not very important for the projects in this book because you knit to the desired length or the specified number of pattern repeats without counting rows.

To measure stitch gauge, place a ruler or tape measure across your swatch horizontally. With pins, mark the beginning and end of a 4-inch (10-cm) section and count the stitches between the pins:

- on garter stitch, count the bumps on the top of the row
- on stockinette stitch, count the Vs across the row

Divide by four to calculate the number of stitches per inch. Check the recommended gauge for your pattern. If your swatch has:

- more stitches per inch than recommended, your swatch is too tight; try again with a larger needle.
- fewer stitches per inch than recommended, your swatch is too loose; try again with a smaller needle.

Tip: *If you are making a scarf, shawl, or other unfitted item and you like the way your swatch looks and drapes, don't worry if the gauge is not an exact match. Your item will not come out the exact size specified in the pattern, but it will be beautiful. Fitted items must match the gauge exactly.*

Lesson and swatch 1:
Practice the basic lace stitches

In this lesson, you will work up a small swatch to practice the basic stitches described on pages 101 to 105. Read the suggestions for Keeping Track of Your Knitting on page 108 before you begin.

Swatch 1. Use worsted-weight wool and 4.5 mm (size 7 U.S.) needles.

1 Cast on 31 stitches.

2 Work 6 rows of garter stitch (knit every row).

3 Set up the chart as follows:

Row 1 (RS): K3, pm, work chart stitches, pm, k3.

Row 2 (WS): K3, sm, purl to next marker, sm, k3.

The three stitches at each end of every row form a garter-stitch border around the center area of lace. Continue to work the chart stitches between the garter-stitch borders, slipping the markers on each row, until all rows of the chart have been worked.

4 Work 6 rows of garter stitch.

5 Bind off all stitches.

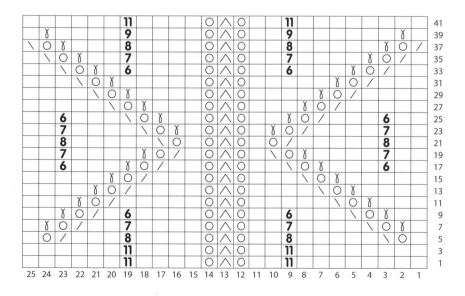

Lesson and swatch 2: Practice a more complex lace chart

In this lesson, you will practice working repeats of a charted pattern. Making a swatch of any new lace pattern is a good habit to get into. Whenever you are ready to learn a new pattern, practice first using a sturdy wool yarn to make sure you can knit the pattern and that you enjoy it. That way you won't waste expensive luxury yarn just to discover you don't like the pattern.

Swatch 2. Use fingering-weight wool yarn on 3.75 mm (size 5 U.S.) needles.

1 Cast on 34 stitches.

2 Work 6 rows of garter stitch (knit every row).

3 Set up the chart as follows:

Row 1 (RS): K3, pm, work chart stitches twice, pm, k3.

Row 2 (WS): K3, sm, purl to next marker, sm, k3.

If you would like, place an extra marker between the chart repeats.

As in swatch 1, the three stitches at each end of every row form a garter-stitch border around the lace pattern. Continue to work the chart stitches between the garter-stitch borders, slipping the markers on each row, until you have worked rows 1 to 6 once and then rows 7 to 26 twice.

4 Work 6 rows of garter stitch.

5 Bind off all stitches.

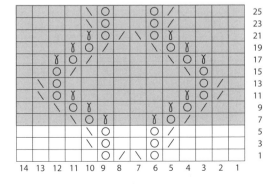

Repeat 20 rows (rows 7–26)

Set-up rows 1–6, work only once

Lesson and swatch 3:
Practice knitting with lace-weight qiviut yarn

In this lesson, you will practice using lace-weight qiviut yarn and will learn how to block your knitting and measure your gauge. You may be tempted to skip this step, but don't. Using a small amount of your precious yarn in this way will ensure that your garment comes out the right size. Making a small investment now will save you time, frustration, and potentially wasted yarn later.

Swatch 3. Use lace-weight qiviut yarn on 3.25 mm (size 3 U.S.) needles.

1 Cast on 34 stitches.

2 Work 6 rows of garter stitch (knit every row).

3 Set up the chart as follows:

Row 1 (RS): K3, pm, work chart stitches, pm, k3.

Row 2 (WS): K3, sm, purl to next marker, sm, k3.

As in swatches 1 and 2, the three stitches at each ends of every row form a garter-stitch border around the lace pattern. Continue to work the chart stitches between the garter-stitch borders, slipping the markers on each row, until all rows of the chart have been worked.

4 Work 6 rows of garter stitch.

5 Bind off all stitches.

6 Wash and block the swatch (see pages 116–117 for blocking instructions).

7 Measure your gauge (see page 111).

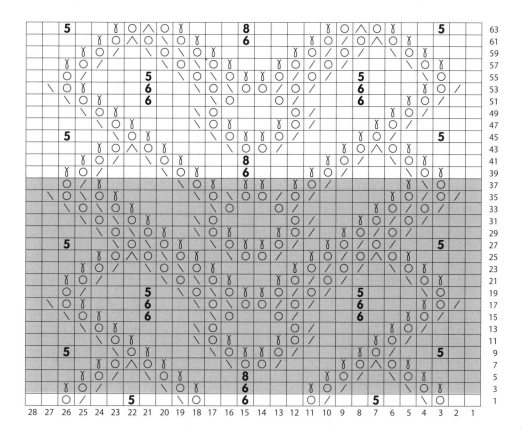

This is the Chevron Scarf chart, also shown on page 139. A repeat is shown, although the repeat information is not required for swatch 3. The bold numbers within the boxes help with stitch-counting in the open areas.

At the beginning of the musk ox recovery efforts, it was almost impossible for spinners and knitters to obtain fiber to work with. Pure qiviut and blends are now available from several suppliers, although sometimes waiting lists form when one year's production has sold out.

Blocking

Blocking is a washing and shaping technique used to make an item match the dimensions specified in the pattern. Blocking finishes the texture of the knitting, smooths out any inconsistencies in gauge, and gives the finished item a professional appearance and a soft drape. Most importantly for lace, when the knitting stretches the yarn-overs open up and the lace pattern becomes more visible and delicate.

I recommend two blocking methods for the projects in this book.

Method 1: Pin and stretch to measurements

Qiviut scarf (top) and a nachaq (bottom) being blocked at the Oomingmak shop in Anchorage.

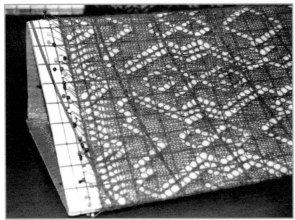

This blocking method is appropriate for scarves and shawls. It stretches the knitting severely, opening up the lace pattern and creating a beautifully light and airy texture. Don't try this on fitted items, however, because it will cause the fabric to lose elasticity.

Qiviut yarn is stretchy when wet, and you can add several inches to the length and width of an item during blocking if desired. If you have substituted yarn of a different fiber in your project, you may not be able to stretch the item to the specified dimensions. Cotton and silk, for example, do not have the elasticity of wool or qiviut, even when wet.

1. Soak the finished item in tepid water until thoroughly wet. I generally leave it for fifteen to thirty minutes. If desired, use a no-rinse wool-washing solution.

2. Gently roll the item in a towel to remove excess water.

3. Lay the item out on a blocking board or other flat surface. At the Oomingmak Co-op, the cutting boards available in fabric stores are used for blocking. These make excellent blocking boards because they are marked with a 1-inch (2.5-cm) grid, making it easy to block to precise measurements and maintain straight edges.

4. Pin the edges of the item to the board. Start with the ends, stretching the item to the desired length. Place a pin in approximately every other stitch. Next pin the sides, placing a pin in each

garter ridge. This is a lot of pins! But if you skimp, the edges will not be straight; they will have undulations like waves where the knitting draws in between the pins.

For a nachaq or other circular item, cut a piece of cardboard to the finished circumference of the item, fold it in thirds to form a triangle, and secure with waterproof tape. Put the nachaq around the blocking triangle and pin in place, stretching the knitting to the desired length.

Method 2: Wash and dry flat

Tip: If you don't want 400 or more rust-proof pins around your house because you have young children or pets, blocking wires are a good substitute. They come in several sizes with detailed instructions. (See page 179 for sources.)

This blocking method is appropriate for fitted garments or any knitting project that includes ribbing.

1. Soak the finished item in tepid water until thoroughly wet (fifteen to thirty minutes). If desired, use a no-rinse wool-washing solution.

2. Gently roll the item in a towel to remove excess water.

3. Place the garment on a flat surface and shape to the dimensions specified in the pattern. If the garment is not perfectly flat, you may decide to pin the edges in place with rust-proof pins. Do not stretch or pin any ribbing because it will lose its elasticity.

Leave the item to dry thoroughly. In arid climates the item may dry in several hours, but even in damp climates, lightweight items should dry overnight. Be patient! Leave the piece pinned for at least twenty-four hours to allow the blocking to set.

Qiviut: Taking care of it

Luxurious and fashionable down fibers and fabrics are also durable and practical. They resist wrinkles and are long-lasting; they become softer with age and rarely pill. If cared for properly, garments knitted from qiviut should last a lifetime.

Take care of garments made from down fibers just as you would other fine woolens. To keep them looking new, handwash in tepid water using a soap for fine washables, and dry flat away from sun or direct heat. (Treat stains as quickly as possible by rinsing immediately with cold water; hot water may set the stain.) When dry, fold the garment and store it flat in a drawer. Never hang handknits on hangers.

To store items over the summer, wash and fold them, and keep them in a chest or drawer with sachets of lavender or eucalyptus to deter moths.

My designs are inspired by the culture and art of the Yup'ik and Inupiat people. I have included projects for new, intermediate, and experienced lace knitters. Many of the items can be made with a small amount of precious yarn.

Chapter 8

Projects

The projects in this chapter provide a backdrop for exploring lace knitting. Just like the designs of the Oomingmak Musk Ox Producers' Co-operative, my designs are inspired by the culture and art of the Yup'ik and Inupiat people.

I've designed projects for knitters of all levels. For new lace knitters, the Lozenge Headband and Fish Trap Hat, Wrist Warmers, and Scarf are made with simple stitch patterns using sport-weight yarn, and the Easy Eyelet Gaiter is made with lace-weight yarn in a simple eyelet design.

If you're ready to expand your lace-knitting skills, the scarves allow you to concentrate on the lace patterning without thinking about shaping. If you prefer knitting in the round, the Skeleton Nachaq Hood and Double-Diamond Fingerless Gloves provide the same opportunity.

If you're already an experienced lace knitter, the Parka-Trim Stole and Grass-Basket Cropped Ruana Vest are larger projects that give you a chance to work with more complicated lace pattern stitches, while the North Star Tam provides an introduction to circular knitting shaped by yarn-overs.

Chart symbols

no stitch (blank)

☐ knit (k), on right side

⊟ purl (p), on right side

⊡ yarn-over (yo)

⊠ knit through back loop (ktbl)

⊘ knit two together (k2tog)

⊠ knit two together through back loop (k2tog-tbl)

⟁ slip one, knit two together, pass slipped stitch over (slip 1, k2tog, psso)

⋁ make one (M1)

* balancing stitch for flat knitting; allows you to center pattern

Unless otherwise noted in instructions, only odd-numbered rows/rounds are shown in the charts. These are the rows/rounds on which the lace patterning is worked.

Unless otherwise noted in instructions, even-numbered rows/rounds are purled in flat knitting and knitted when working in the round, producing a stockinette-stitch ground for the lace.

Photo opposite by Dominic Cotignola.

Lozenge Headband

I love fast and easy projects for learning new techniques and trying new yarns. This headband requires less than one ounce (usually one ball) of qiviut yarn and is small enough to complete in a weekend. I adapted the Lozenge pattern from the decoration on a Yup'ik sewing kit. The simple pattern introduces the main stitches used in lace knitting, so this is a good starting project for new lace knitters.

Instructions

1 Cast on 12 stitches. Knit 11 rows of garter stitch, flat (knit all rows).

2 Work increases:

Set-up row (WS): K3, place marker (pm), p6, pm, k3.

Row 1 (RS): K3, slip marker (sm), m1, knit to 2nd marker, m1, sm, k3.

Row 2 (WS): K3, sm, p to 2nd marker, sm, k3.

Repeat rows 1 and 2 until you have 14 stitches between markers—20 stitches total.

3 Set up pattern:

Row 1 (RS): K3, sm, work Lozenge pattern (chart opposite), sm, k3.

Row 2 (WS): K3, sm, p to 2nd marker (but knit into the second yarn-over of each double yarn-over), sm, k3.

4 Pattern: Continue working pattern as established, slipping markers when you come to them, until you have completed 6 (7, 8) repeats of Lozenge pattern.

5 Work decreases:

Row 1 (RS): K3, sm, ssk, knit to 2 stitches before 2nd marker, k2tog, sm, k3.

Row 2 (WS): K3, sm, purl to 2nd marker, sm, k3.

Repeat rows 1 and 2 until a total of 12 stitches remain.

6 Finish: Knit 10 rows. Bind off.

Sew ends of headband together. weave in ends.

The inspiration for the pattern on this headband came from the design on a pouch that I discovered in the Museum of the North, at the University of Alaska in Fairbanks.

Tobacco pouch from the University of Alaska Museum of the North Collection, catalog number 64-21-862. Used by permission. Photo by Angela Linn.

Lozenge Headband	
Sizes	S (M, L)
Knitted measurements	Approx. 3 x 17 (19, 21) inches (7.5 x 43 [48, 53.5] cm), blocked
Skill level	Easy
Gauge	6 stitches = 1 inch (2.5 cm) in stockinette stitch, blocked
Needles	3.25 mm / 3 U.S.
Yarn	130 yards (119 m) sport-weight yarn
The yarn I used	Folknits Sport Weight Qiviuq, Natural 100% qiviuq 130 yards (119 m) per 25-g (.9-ounce) skein 1 skein

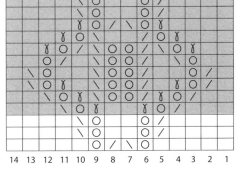

Pattern stitch for Lozenge Headband

LOZENGE PATTERN

Worked flat on stockinette-stitch ground; purl even-numbered (wrong-side/WS) rows.

Repeat (shaded area): 20 rows x 14 stitches.

On the return (wrong-side/WS) row after a double yarn-over, purl into the first yarn-over and knit into the second yarn-over (see page 103).

Set-up rows 1–6, work only once

Fish Trap Hat, Wrist Warmers, and Scarf

This set of accessories allows you to practice following an easy lace chart. The hat and wrist warmers are knitted in the round with sport-weight qiviut, and the scarf is knitted back and forth in lace-weight cashmere. This simple design with parallel lines reminds me of the wood-splint fish traps and grass fish bags that the Yup'ik people once used.

Instructions for hat

1 With circular needles, cast on 120 (130) stitches. Place marker. Join and knit in the round.

2 Work 8 rounds of garter stitch, circular:

Round 1 and all odd rounds: Knit.

Round 2 and all even rounds: Purl.

3 Work Fish Trap (circular) pattern (chart on page 124) until hat measures 5 inches (12.5 cm) from cast-on edge or desired height to crown.

4 Shape crown. Change to double-pointed needles when the stitches no longer fit on the circular needle. Shaping for size L begins with round 1. Shaping for size M begins with round 3.

Round 1 (size M only): Knit.

Round 1 (size L only): (K11, k2tog) around (total 120 stitches).

Round 2 and all even rounds: Knit.

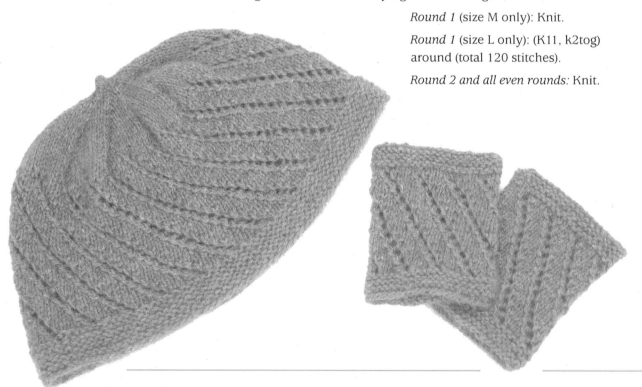

Round 3: (K8, k2tog) around (total 108 stitches).

Round 5: (K7, k2tog) around (total 96 stitches).

Round 7: (K6, k2tog) around (total 84 stitches).

Round 9: (K5, k2tog) around (total 72 stitches).

Round 11: (K4, k2tog) around (total 60 stitches).

Round 13: (K3, k2tog) around (total 48 stitches).

Round 15: (K2, k2tog) around (total 36 stitches).

Round 17: (K1, k2tog) around (total 24 stitches).

Rounds 19, 21, and 23: K2tog around—3 stitches remain after round 23.

5 Work 3-stitch I-cord on two double-pointed needles as follows:

K3, do not turn. Slide stitches to the other end of needle.

Repeat until I-cord measures ½ inch (1.3 cm).

Cut yarn.

FINISHING

Draw tail through remaining 3 stitches and fasten off.

Weave in ends.

The pattern on this warm set of accessories was inspired by wooden fish traps.

Photo courtesy of Alaska State Library, Historical Collections, Juneau. Used by permission. Best trap-maker in the village. Kalskag, Alaska, February 1940.

Fish Trap Hat	
Sizes	Adult M (L)
Knitted measurements	20 (21.5) inches (51 [55] cm) circumference
Skill level	Easy
Gauge	6 stitches = 1 inch (2.5 cm) in stockinette stitch, as knitted
Needles	3.25 mm / 3 U.S.—16 inches (40 cm) or 20 inches (50 cm) long 3.25 mm / 3 U.S.—set of four or five double-pointed needles
Yarn	130+ yards (119 m) sport-weight yarn (see note)
The yarn I used	Folknits Sport Weight Qiviuq, Natural 100% qiviuq 130 yards (117 m) per 25-g (.9-ounce) skein 1+ skein (see note)

Note: This hat requires just over 1 skein or 130+ yards of yarn. If you get 2 skeins or 260 yards, you will have enough to make both the hat and the matching wrist warmers.

Pattern stitch for Fish Trap Hat and Wrist Warmers

FISH TRAP PATTERN (CIRCULAR)

Worked in the round on a stockinette-stitch ground; knit even-numbered rounds.

Repeat (shaded area): 10 rounds x 5 stitches.

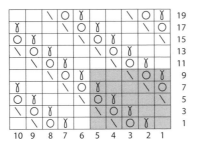

Pattern stitch for Fish Trap Scarf

FINE FISH TRAP PATTERN

Worked flat on stockinette-stitch ground; purl even-numbered (wrong-side/WS) rows.

Repeat (shaded area): 12 rows x 6 stitches.

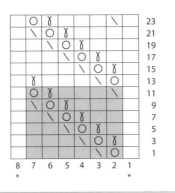

Instructions for wrist warmers

Note: *Make two identical wrist warmers.*

1 With smaller needles, cast on 45 (50) stitches. Place marker. Join and knit in the round.

2 Work 6 rounds of garter stitch (circular):

   Round 1 and all odd rounds: Knit.

   Round 2 and all even rounds: Purl.

3 Change to larger needles. Work Fish Trap pattern (circular) until piece measures 2 ½ inches (6.4 cm) from cast-on edge, or ½ inch (1.3 cm) shorter than desired.

4 Change to smaller needles. Work 6 rounds of garter stitch (circular), as in step 2.

Bind off loosely. Cut yarn.

FINISHING

Weave in ends.

Fish Trap Wrist Warmers	
Sizes	Adult M (L)
Knitted measurements	7 (8) inches (18 [20.5] cm) circumference (these are stretchy)
Skill level	Easy
Gauge	6½ stitches = 1 inch (2.5 cm) in pattern stitch on larger needles, as knitted
Needles	2.75 mm / 2 U.S.—set of four or five double-pointed needles 3.25 mm / 3 U.S.—set of four or five double-pointed needles
Yarn	130 yards (119 m) sport-weight yarn (see note)
The yarn I used	Folknits Sport Weight Qiviuq, Natural 100% qiviuq 130 yards (117 m) per 25-g (.9-ounce) skein 1 skein (see note)
Note: The wrist warmers require slightly less than 1 skein or 130 yards of yarn. See also note for Fish Trap Hat on page 123.	

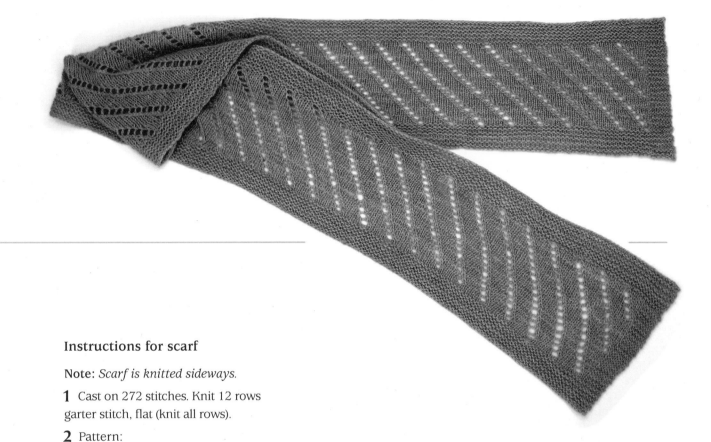

Instructions for scarf

Note: *Scarf is knitted sideways.*

1 Cast on 272 stitches. Knit 12 rows garter stitch, flat (knit all rows).

2 Pattern:

Row 1 (RS): K6, pm, work Fine Fish Trap pattern to last 6 stitches, pm, k6.

Row 2 (WS): K6, sm, purl to 2nd marker, sm, k6.

Continue pattern as established, slipping markers when you come to them, until scarf measures 4 inches (10 cm) from cast-on edge. End after working a wrong-side row.

3 Knit 12 rows garter stitch, flat. Bind off loosely.

FINISHING

Weave in ends and block.

Fish Trap Scarf	
Sizes	One size
Knitted measurements	Approx. 5 x 46 inches (13 x 117 cm), blocked
Skill level	Easy
Gauge	6 stitches = 1 inch (2.5 cm) in stockinette stitch, blocked
Needles	3.25 mm / 3 U.S.
Yarn	300 yards (274 m) lace-weight yarn
The yarn I used	Look China, 100 percent Cashmere Yarn, Natural Creamy White 100 percent cashmere 1000 yards (914 m) in 5-ounce (142-g) skein 1 skein

North Star Tam and Scarf

The North Star is a classic symbol of Alaska. This tam and scarf are both made with lace-weight 100 percent qiviut yarn. Both the scarf and the sides of the tam are decorated with star motifs. The scarf, knitted back and forth, is less challenging than the tam.

If you have some experience knitting lace, you will find the tam pattern exciting. Starting in the center with just eight stitches and working in the round, you increase with yarn-overs to form a beautiful circular lace star on its crown.

The tam is shown here in lace-weight qiviut. It is also shown in fingering-weight wool on page 4.

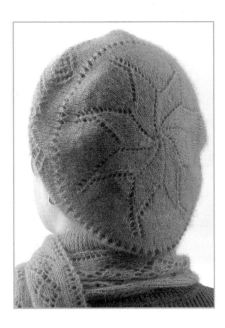

Instructions for tam

CROWN

1 Cast on 8 stitches. Place marker. Join and knit in the round. Knit 1 round.

2 Work lace increases from instructions below or follow Tam Center Star pattern (chart on page 128):

Begin star pattern:

Round 1: (Yo, k1) around (total 16 stitches).

Round 2 and all even rounds: Knit.

Round 3: (Yo, k2) around (total 24 stitches).

Round 5: (Yo, k3) around (total 32 stitches).

Round 7: (Yo, k4) around (total 40 stitches).

Round 9: (Yo, k5) around (total 48 stitches).

Round 11: (Yo, k6) around (total 56 stitches).

Round 13: (Yo, k7) around (total 64 stitches).

Round 15: (Yo, k8) around (total 72 stitches).

Round 17: (Yo, k9) around (total 80 stitches).

Round 19: (K7, k2tog, yo, k1, yo) around (total 88 stitches).

Round 21: (K6, k2tog, yo, k3, yo) around (total 96 stitches).

Round 23: (K5, k2tog, yo, k5, yo) around (total 104 stitches).

Round 25: (K4, k2tog, yo, k7, yo) around (total 112 stitches).

Round 27: (K3, k2tog, yo, k9, yo) around (total 120 stitches).

Round 29: (K2, k2tog, yo, k11, yo) around (total 128 stitches).

Round 31: (K1, k2tog, yo, k13, yo) around (total 136 stitches).

Round 33: (K2tog, yo, k15, yo) around (total 144 stitches).

Continue, working each odd round as (k2tog, yo, knit 1 more stitch than in previous round, yo) around until you have 176 stitches.

North Star Tam	
Sizes	Adult medium
Knitted measurements	18 inches (45.7 cm) circumference at ribbing
Skill level	Advanced
Gauge	8 stitches x 10 rows = 1 inch (2.5 cm) in stockinette stitch as knitted
Needles	2.25 mm / 1 U.S.—16 inches (40 cm) or 20 inches (50 cm) long 2.25 mm / 1 U.S.—set of four or five double-pointed needles
Yarn	300 yards (274 m) lace-weight yarn
The yarn I used	Nash Farm Alaska Qiviuk, Gold Rush 100 percent qiviuk 220 yards (202 m) in 1-ounce (28.5-g) ball 2 balls

SIDES

1 Work Eyelet Band pattern:

Rounds 1 to 6: Knit.

Round 7: (K2tog, yo) around.

Rounds 8 to 13: Knit.

2 Work all rounds of Small North Star pattern (48 rounds).

3 Work rounds 1 to 13 of Eyelet Band pattern, as in step 1.

Pattern stitches for North Star Tam

TAM CENTER STAR PATTERN

Worked in the round on a stockinette-stitch ground; knit even-numbered rounds.

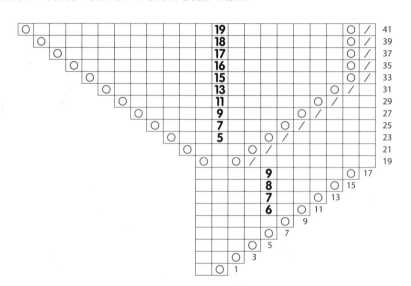

SMALL NORTH STAR PATTERN

Worked in the round on a stockinette-stitch ground; knit even-numbered rounds.

The bold numbers within the boxes help with stitch-counting in the open areas. They include only the stitches inside the horizontal repeat.

RIBBING

1 Knit one round, decreasing 56 stitches evenly around as follows:

*K2, (k2, k2tog) 14 times. Repeat from * to end of round (total 120 stitches).

2 Work in Twisted Ribbing for 1 inch (2.5 cm):

Round 1: (Ktbl, p1) around.

Repeat round 1 for pattern.

3 Bind off loosely.

FINISHING

Weave in ends and block over a dinner plate.

Instructions for scarf

1 Cast on 63 stitches. Knit 4 rows (garter stitch, flat).

2 Patterns (charts on page 130):

Row 1 (RS): Work Right Eyelet Edging #1, pm, work North Star with Diamonds, pm, work Left Eyelet Edging #1.

Row 2 (WS): K4, sm, purl to 2nd marker, sm, k4.

Continue patterns as established, slipping markers when you come to them, until you have completed 9 repeats of the North Star pattern. End after working a wrong-side row.

3 Knit 4 rows (garter stitch, flat). Bind off loosely.

FINISHING

Weave in ends and block.

North Star Scarf	
Sizes	One size
Knitted measurements	10 x 60 inches (25.5 x 152.5 cm), blocked
Skill level	Intermediate
Gauge	7 stitches = 1 inch (2.5 cm) in stockinette stitch, blocked
Needles	3.25 mm / 3 U.S.
Yarn	420 yards (384 m) lace-weight yarn
The yarn I used	Nash Farm Alaska Qiviuk, Gold Rush 100 percent qiviuk 220 yards (202 m) in 1-ounce (28.5-g) ball 2 balls

Pattern stitches for
North Star Scarf

NORTH STAR WITH
DIAMONDS PATTERN

Chart at right; begins on next page and continues on this page.

Worked flat on stockinette-stitch ground; purl even-numbered (wrong-side/WS) rows.

Repeat: 56 rows x 55 stitches.

Chart continued from page 131 ←

LEFT EYELET EDGING #1

Worked flat on garter-stitch ground; knit even-numbered (wrong-side/WS) rows.

Repeat: 2 rows x 4 stitches.

RIGHT EYELET EDGING #1

Worked flat on garter-stitch ground; knit even-numbered (wrong-side/WS) rows.

Repeat: 2 rows x 4 stitches.

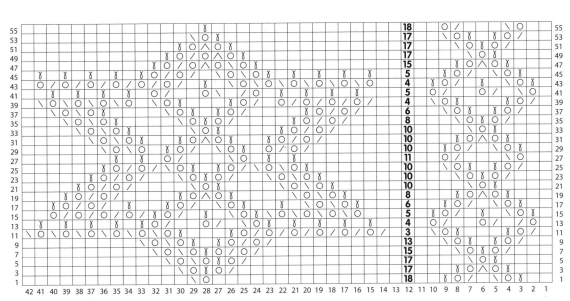

← *Chart continues on page 130*

The bold numbers within the boxes
help with stitch-counting in the open
areas. They include only the stitches
inside the horizontal repeat.

Skeleton Scarf and Nachaq Hood

The designs on this scarf and nachaq hood are inspired by the paintings of skeletons on many Yup'ik wooden utensils and boxes. The scarf is knitted back and forth with a slip-stitch selvedge; the nachaq is knitted in the round. If you want to compare working the same pattern both ways, these are excellent practice projects. The scarf, made with just one ounce of qiviut, would make an extravagant gift. The nachaq, which takes more yarn, may be the perfect project to pamper yourself. (Or vice versa.)

Instructions for scarf

Note: *To form selvedge, slip the first stitch and knit the last stitch of every row for entire scarf.*

1 Cast on 65 stitches.

2 Work Double Eyelet Column pattern (chart on page 134):

Row 1 (RS): Slip 1 (selvedge stitch), k3, sm, work Double Eyelet Column pattern to last 4 stitches, sm, k3, k1 (selvedge stitch).

Row 2 (WS): Slip 1, k3, sm, purl to 2nd marker, sm, k3, k1.

Continue working pattern as established, slipping markers when you come to them, until you have completed 26 rows of Double Eyelet Column pattern.

3 Work garter ridge with increases:

Row 1 (RS): Slip 1 (selvedge stitch), *k3, m1, k27, m1, rep from * once more, k3, k1 (selvedge stitch) (total 69 stitches).

Rows 2, 3, and 4: Slip 1, knit to last stitch, k1.

4 Work Skeleton pattern, flat (chart on page 135):

Row 1 (RS): Slip 1, k3, sm, work Skeleton pattern to last 4 stitches, sm, k3, k1. As noted on the chart, the Skeleton pattern repeat of 61 stitches consists of stitches 1 through 32 followed by stitches 1 through 29.

Row 2 (WS): Slip 1, k3, sm, purl to 2nd marker, sm, k3, k1.

Continue pattern as established, slipping markers when you come to them, until you have completed 3 repeats of the Skeleton pattern. End after working row 92.

5 Work garter ridge with decreases:

Row 1: Slip 1, *k3, k2tog, k27, k2tog, rep from * once more, k3, k1 (total 65 stitches).

Rows 2, 3, and 4: Slip 1, knit to last stitch, k1.

I first saw a photo of this spoon in a book I'd taken out of the library. I was thrilled to see it for real when I went to Alaska. It was in the collection of the Museum of the North at the University of Alaska in Fairbanks.

Photo © Dominic Cotignola. Wooden spoon with animal figure depicted in X-ray vision style, from the University of Alaska Museum of the North Collection, catalog number UA94-009-0030. Used by permission.

Skeleton Scarf	
Sizes	One size
Knitted measurements	9 x 40 inches (23 x 101.5 cm), blocked
Skill level	Intermediate
Gauge	Approx. 7 stitches = 1 inch (2.5 cm) in stockinette stitch, blocked
Needles	3.25 mm / 3 U.S.
Yarn	320 yards (293 m) extra-fine lace-weight yarn
The yarn I used	Robert G. White Large Animal Research Station (LARS) Qiviut, Natural 100 percent qiviut 320 yards (293 m) in 1-ounce (28.5-g) skein 1 skein

6 Work 26 rows of Double Eyelet Column pattern (as in step 2 on pages 132–133).

Bind off loosely.

Border pattern for Skeleton Scarf and Nachaq Hood

DOUBLE EYELET COLUMN PATTERN

Worked on stockinette-stitch ground.

For flat knitting (scarf), repeat stitches 1 through 5 across and balance at end with stitches marked *. Purl even-numbered (wrong-side/WS) rows.

Repeat: 2 rows x 5 stitches (+ 2 stitches to balance).

For circular knitting (nachaq hood), repeat stitches 1 through 5 around. Knit even-numbered rounds.

Repeat: 2 rows x 5 stitches.

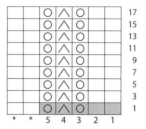

Skeleton Nachaq Hood	
Sizes	One size
Knitted measurements	22 x 18 inches (56 x 46 cm), blocked
Skill level	Intermediate
Gauge	Approx. 8 stitches = 1 inch (2.5 cm) in stockinette stitch, blocked
Needles	2.75 mm / 2 U.S.—16 inches (40 cm) or 20 inches (50 cm) long.
Yarn	650 yards (594 m) extra-fine lace-weight yarn
The yarn I used.	Folknits Extra Fine Lace Weight Qiviuq, Natural 100 percent qiviuq 270 yards (248 m) in 25-g (.9-ounce) skein 3 skeins

FINISHING

Weave in ends and block.

Instructions for nachaq hood

1 Cast on 180 stitches. Place marker and join to knit in the round.

2 Work 26 rounds of Double Eyelet Column pattern, circular (chart at left).

3 Work garter ridge with increases:

Round 1: *M1, k27, m1, k3, rep from * five more times—192 stitches total.

Rounds 2 and 4: Purl.

Round 3: Knit.

4 Pattern:

Round 1: Work Skeleton pattern, circular (chart opposite), placing markers between pattern repeats.

Round 2: Knit.

Continue pattern as established, slipping markers when you come to them, until you have completed 2 repeats of the Skeleton pattern. End after working row 92.

5 Work garter ridge with decreases:

Round 1: *K2tog, k27, k2tog, k3, rep from * five more times—180 stitches total.

Rounds 2 and 4: Purl.

Round 3: Knit.

6 Work 26 rounds of Double Eyelet Column pattern, circular, as in step 2.

Bind off loosely.

FINISHING

Weave in ends and block.

Body pattern for Skeleton Scarf and Nachaq Hood

SKELETON PATTERN

Worked on stockinette-stitch ground.

For flat knitting (scarf), work stitches 1 through 32 and then repeat stitches 1 through 29 once. Purl even-numbered (wrong-side/WS) rows.

Repeat: 92 rows x 61 stitches.

For circular knitting (nachaq hood), repeat stitches 1 through 32 around (there will be 6 repeats of 32 stitches in the nachaq body). Knit even-numbered rounds.

Repeat: 92 rounds x 32 stitches.

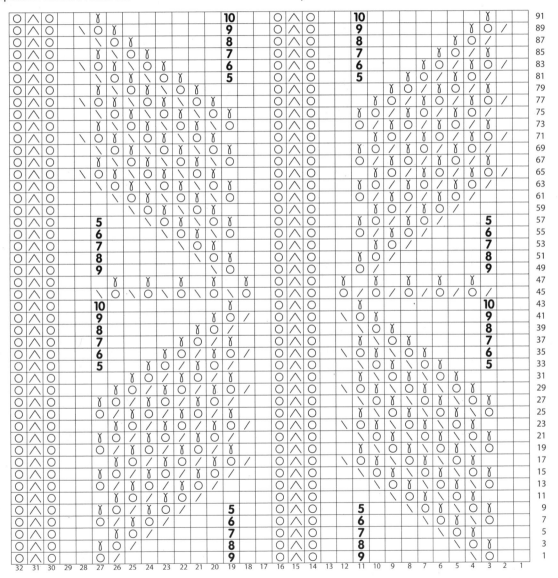

The bold numbers within the boxes help with stitch-counting in the open areas. They include only the stitches inside the horizontal repeat.

Chevron Scarf

I adapted the chevron designs in this scarf from carvings on Yup'ik and Inupiat ivory tools and the basket opposite. My favorite pieces are the ornately carved needle cases that Inupiat women kept in their sewing kits. The scarf has three stitch patterns: a simple eyelet edging, a small chevron border on both ends, and a large chevron design that makes up the body of the scarf. Because the chevron design looks best going a single direction, I made this scarf in two pieces, so the design would face the center from both ends.

Instructions

Note: *Scarf is made in two pieces. Stitches are cast on at the end and knitted to the center. Pieces are grafted together with Kitchener stitch (see page 107).*

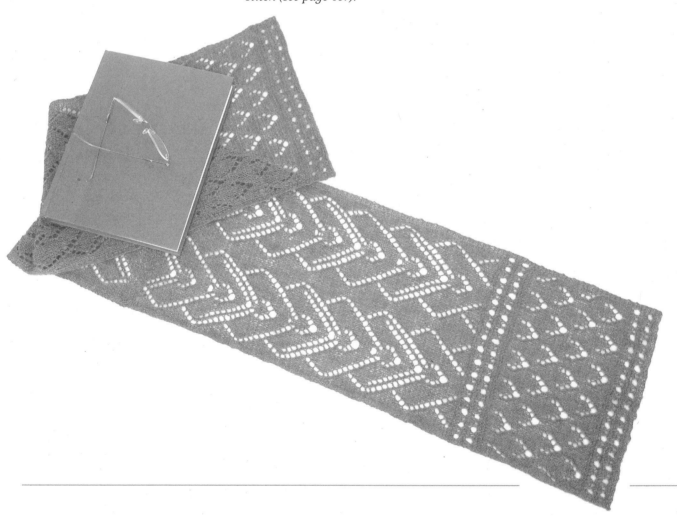

1 Cast on 64 stitches.

2 Work 16 rows of Eyelet Garter Ridge (chart on page 138), increasing 2 stitches evenly across on last row: (K21, m1) two times, k22 (total 66 stitches).

3 Mini-Chevron Border (chart on page 138):

Row 1 (RS): K3, pm, work Mini-Chevron Border pattern until 3 stitches remain, pm, k3.

Row 2 (WS): K3, sm, purl to 2nd marker (but knit into the second yarn-over of each double yarn-over), sm, k3.

Continue pattern as established, slipping markers when you come to them, until you have completed row 40 of the Mini-Chevron Border pattern.

4 Work 16 rows of Eyelet Garter Ridge, decreasing 2 stitches evenly across first row—(k21, k2tog) two times, k20 (total 64 stitches)—and decreasing 2 stitches evenly across last row—(k20, k2tog) two times, k20 (total 62 stitches).

5 Chevron pattern for body (chart on page 139):

Row 1 (RS): K3, sm, work Chevron pattern until 3 stitches remain, sm, k3.

Row 2 (WS): K3, sm, purl to 2nd marker (but knit into the second yarn-over of each double yarn-over), sm, k3.

Continue working patterns as established, slipping markers when you come to them. Work rows 1 through 38 of Chevron pattern once, then rows 3 through 38 twice. Complete pattern by working rows 39 through 64 once.

Do not bind off. Place stitches on holder.

Make a second, identical piece.

FINISHING

Graft the two pieces together using Kitchener stitch.

Weave in ends and block.

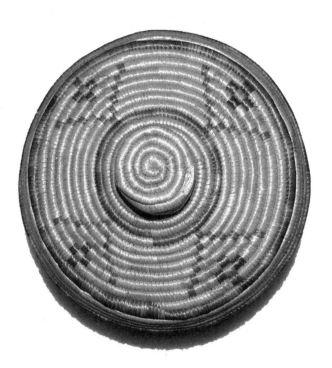

The large and small motifs on the Chevron Scarf were inspired by the patterning on this grass basket.

Photo © Dominic Cotignola. Coiled grass basket from the University of Alaska Museum of the North Collection, catalog number UA71-16-46B. Used by permission.

Chevron Scarf	
Sizes	One size
Knitted measurements	11 x 50 inches (28 x 127 cm), blocked
Skill level	Intermediate
Gauge	6 stitches = 1 inch (2.5 cm) in stockinette stitch, blocked
Needles	3.25 mm / 3 U.S.
Yarn	420 yards (385 m) lace-weight yarn
The yarn I used	Folknits Regular Lace Weight Qiviuq, Natural 100 percent qiviuq 210 yards (193 m) in 25-g (.9-ounce) skein 2 skeins

Pattern stitches for Chevron Scarf

(see also next page)

EYELET GARTER RIDGE PATTERN

Worked flat on garter-stitch ground; knit even-numbered (wrong-side/WS) rows.

Repeat (shaded area): 6 rows x 4 stitches. (Chart goes all the way to the edges of the fabric.)

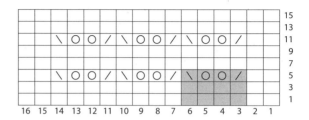

MINI-CHEVRON BORDER PATTERN

Worked flat on stockinette-stitch ground; purl even-numbered rows.

Repeat (shaded area): 40 rows x 10 stitches. (Three stitches at each edge, not included in chart, are in garter stitch.)

For both patterns:

On the return (wrong-side) row after a double yarn-over, purl into the first yarn-over and knit into the second yarn-over (see page 103).

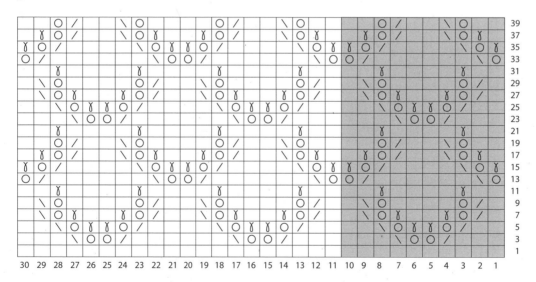

Pattern stitches for Chevron Scarf

(see also previous page)

CHEVRON PATTERN

Worked flat on stockinette-stitch ground; purl even-numbered (wrong-side/WS) rows.

Repeat (shaded area, rows 3 through 38): 36 rows x 28 stitches. Complete pattern at end of scarf with rows 39 through 64.

On the return (wrong-side) row after a double yarn-over, purl into the first yarn-over and knit into the second yarn-over (see page 103).

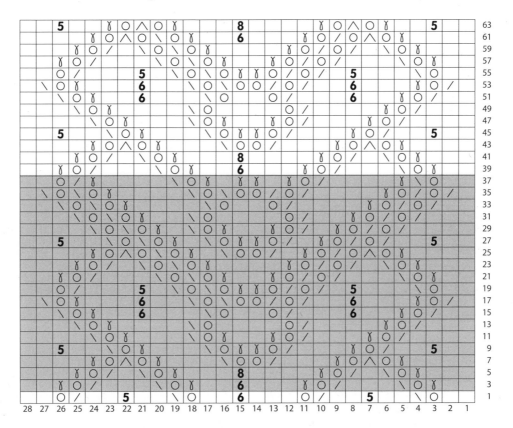

The bold numbers within the boxes help with stitch-counting in the open areas. They include only the stitches inside the horizontal repeat.

Möbius Scarf

Because I wanted to make a reversible möbius scarf, I used garter stitch for the background. Therefore I knitted the wrong-side rows, even though the scarf is worked flat. The stitch pattern would be slightly more obvious with a stockinette-stitch background, and you can easily adapt this design to make a straight scarf with a smooth, stockinette ground. The stitch pattern is from Dorothy Reade's book, *25 Original Knitting Designs.* The curving shapes remind me of the scooped hems on many old-style Yup'ik and Inupiat women's parkas, a shape that was mirrored in the decorations on many other personal items for women.

Instructions

1 Cast on 69 stitches. Knit 2 rows.

2 Patterns (charts on page 142):

Row 1 (RS): Work Right Eyelet Edging, pm, work Scoop-Hem Parka pattern, pm, work Left Eyelet Edging.

Row 2 (WS): Knit.

Continue patterns as established, slipping markers when you come to them, until scarf is approx. 50 inches (127 cm) long and you have just a few yards of yarn remaining. End after working either row 7 or row 15 of the Scoop-Hem Parka pattern.

3 Knit 1 row. Bind off.

FINISHING

Weave in ends and block.

Join ends together, putting a half-twist into the scarf before you sew the seam.

The inspiration for the pattern on the Möbius Scarf came from the scooped hemlines on women's traditional parkas, shown above.

Women standing on ice at Tanana. Photo © Archives, Alaska and Polar Regions Collections, Rasmuson Library, University of Alaska Fairbanks. Used by permission.

Möbius Scarf	
Sizes	One size
Knitted measurements	10 x 50 inches (25.5 x 127 cm), blocked
Skill level	Intermediate
Gauge	7 stitches = 1 inch (2.5 cm) in stockinette stitch, blocked
Needles	3.25 mm / 3 U.S.
Yarn	approximately 500 yards (460 m) extra-fine lace-weight yarn
The yarn I used	100 percent qiviut about 750 yards (690 m) in 2-ounce (57-g) skein 1 skein

Note: I used yarn that I picked up at a yarn shop in Anchorage, Alaska. The yarn had no label on it and I wasn't able to find out anything more about it. It was the finest yarn of any that I used. Based on feel in comparison to the other yarns, I estimate that there were at least 350 yards in an ounce. I knitted until the skein was almost gone, being sure to complete a pattern repeat, and then assembled the scarf. Any of the lace-weight yarns used in this book will make a beautiful möbius scarf.

Pattern stitches for Möbius Scarf

SCOOP-HEM PARKA PATTERN

Worked flat on garter-stitch ground; knit even-numbered (wrong-side/WS) rows.

Repeat: 8 rows x 20 stitches; note treatment of edge and center decreases.

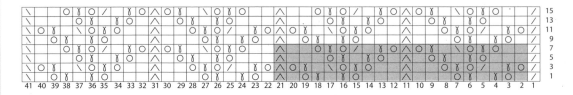

LEFT EYELET EDGING #1

Worked flat on garter-stitch ground; knit even-numbered (wrong-side/WS) rows.

Repeat: 2 rows x 4 stitches.

RIGHT EYELET EDGING #1

Worked flat on garter-stitch ground; knit even-numbered (wrong-side/WS) rows.

Repeat: 2 rows x 4 stitches.

Give the completed fabric a half-twist
before sewing the ends together.

Completed fabric

Half-twist

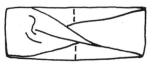

Sew the ends together

Parka-Trim Stole

This stole, featuring a diamond pattern inspired by the trim on parkas, is as easy to make as a scarf. It is so luxurious and soft that you will want to wrap it around yourself while you read in bed. But if you decide to wear it for holiday parties and weddings, you can show it off and be the best-dressed person at the event. I would make a second stole out of less-expensive merino wool yarn to wear for lounging. (You can easily convert any of the scarves in this book to stoles by adding additional repeats in width and length.)

*This stole, or any other, can
be stitched as shown above to form a poncho.
One short end is seamed to one of the long sides.*

Instructions

Note: *The beginning and ending of the stole have slight differences in the Eyelet Edging.*

1 Cast on 130 stitches.

2 Work Beginning Eyelet Edging (on garter-stitch background):

Rows 1 (WS) through 5: Knit.

Row 6 (RS): K1, *yo, k2tog. Repeat from * to last stitch. End yo, k1—131 stitches.

Row 7 (WS): Knit.

Row 8 (RS): *K2tog, yo. Repeat from * to last stitch. End k1.

Rows 9 through 12: Knit.

Row 13 (WS): Knit.

3 Set up pattern:

Row 1 (RS): K3, pm, work five repeats of Parka-Trim Diamond pattern, pm, k3.

Row 2 and all even rows (WS): K3, sm, purl to 2nd marker, sm, k3.

4 Pattern:

Continue working pattern as established, slipping markers when you come to them. Work rows 1 to 10 of Parka-Trim Diamond chart once (bottom set-up rows), rows 11 to 74 nine times (repeats), and rows 75 to 101 once (complete final section of pattern; the last pattern row is a RS row).

5 Work Ending Eyelet Edging (on garter-stitch background):

Rows 1 (WS) *through 5:* Knit.

Row 6 (RS): *K2tog, yo. Repeat from * to last stitch. End k1.

Row 7 (WS): Knit.

Row 8 (RS): K1, *yo, k2tog. Repeat from * to last stitch.

Rows 9 through13: Knit.

Bind off loosely.

FINISHING

Weave in ends and block.

While in Alaska, I saw skin-sewers making diamond parka-trim like this out of tiny pieces of fur. That was the inspiration for this stole.

Photo © Clark James Mishler. Used by permission.

Parka-Trim Stole	
Sizes	One size
Knitted measurements	18 x 70 inches (46 x 178 cm), blocked
Skill level	Intermediate
Gauge	7 stitches = 1 inch (2.5 cm), blocked
Needles	3.25 mm / 3 U.S.
Yarn	1620 yards (1481 m) extra-fine lace-weight yarn
The yarn I used	Folknits Extra Fine Lace Weight Qiviuq, Natural 100 percent qiviuq 270 yards (248 m) in 25-g (.9-ounce) skein 6 skeins

Pattern stitch for Parka-Trim Stole

**PARKA-TRIM
DIAMOND PATTERN**

Worked flat on
stockinette-stitch ground;
purl even-numbered
(wrong-side/WS) rows.

Repeat (inside box): 64
rows x 25 stitches.

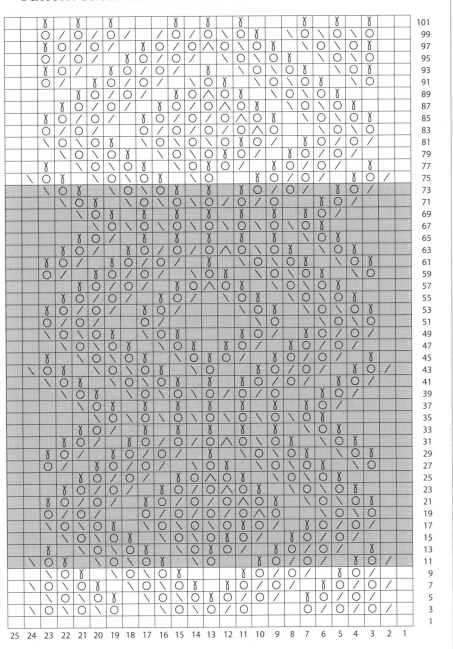

Grass-Basket Cropped Ruana Vest

This vest is a perfect palette for knitted lace. Because it has little shaping, you can concentrate on the stitch patterns without worrying about maintaining the design while you shape the armholes and neck. The stitch pattern is adapted from a Yup'ik grass basket. I changed the single design into a pattern that repeats and interlocks over the entire body of the vest. The fronts and back are knitted together until you reach the armholes, so there are no side seams to interrupt the design.

Instructions

Note: *Fronts and back are worked together to armholes. Throughout body, knit first and last stitches of every row to form selvedges. See page 148 for charts.*

LOWER BODY

1 Cast on 298 stitches.

2 Set-up row (WS):

K1 (selvedge stitch), *k2, p5. Rep from * to last 3 stitches, k2, k1 (selvedge stitch).

3 Pattern—ribbing:

Row 1 (RS): K1 (selvedge stitch), work Double Eyelet Ribbing repeat to last 3 stitches, p2 (balancing stitches), k1 (selvedge stitch).

Row 2 (WS): K1 (selvedge stitch), k2 (balancing stitches), *p5, k2, repeat from * across to last stitch, k1 (selvedge stitch).

Continue pattern as established until piece measures 4 inches (10 cm). End with a wrong-side row.

4 Work Garter Ridge pattern: Knit 6 rows; in last row of pattern, decrease 1 stitch (total 297 stitches).

5 Pattern—body:

Row 1 (RS): K1 (selvedge stitch), work Grass-Basket pattern stitches 1 to 43 once, then stitches 2 to 43 six times, k1 (selvedge stitch).

Row 2 (WS): K1 (selvedge stitch), purl across to last stitch, k1 (selvedge stitch).

Continue pattern as established until piece measures 7 (8) inches (17.8 [20.3] cm).

End after a wrong-side row.

6 Divide for armholes, continuing pattern as established:

Work 64 stitches (left front). Place stitches on holder.

Bind off one stitch. Work 167 stitches (back). Place stitches on holder.

Bind off one stitch. Work 64 stitches (right front).

RIGHT FRONT

1 Work only on right front stitches and continue to knit first and last stitches of every row for selvedge:

Continue in Grass-Basket pattern as established until a total of 4 pattern repeats have been completed and front measures approx. 20 (22) inches (51 [56] cm) from cast-on edge.

2 Begin neck shaping:

At neck edge, increase 1 stitch every right-side row 12 times, working increases in stockinette stitch.

End after a wrong-side row.

3 Work Garter Ridge pattern: Knit 6 rows.

Do not bind off. Cut yarn, leaving enough yarn attached to work three-needle bind-off to join shoulder.

BACK

1 Work only on back stitches and continue to knit first and last stitches of every row for selvedge:

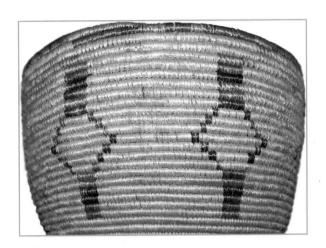

The inspiration for the pattern on the Grass-Basket Cropped Ruana Vest came from this Yup'ik grass basket from the Museum of the North at the University of Alaska Fairbanks.

Photo © Dominic Cotignola. Basket with diamond pattern, from the University of Alaska Museum of the North Collection, catalog number 322-47. Used by permission.

Work even in Grass-Basket pattern as established until back measures same as right front to Garter Ridge pattern.

End after a wrong-side row.

2 Work Garter Ridge pattern: Knit 6 rows.

Do not bind off. Cut yarn.

Grass-Basket Cropped Ruana Vest	
Sizes	S/M (L/XL)
Knitted measurements	Circumference (buttoned): 42 (49) inches (107 [124.5] cm), Length: 20 (22) inches (51 [55.8] cm)
Skill level	Advanced
Gauge	7 (6) stitches = 1 inch (2.5 cm), as knitted
Needles	3.25 mm / 3 U.S. (3.5 mm / 4 U.S.)
Yarn	1182 (1379) yards (1081 [1261] m) lace-weight yarn
The yarn I used	Folknits Regular Lace Weight Qiviuq Blend, Light Natural 45 percent qiviuq, 45 percent wool, 10 percent silk 197 yards (180 m) in 25-g (.9-ounce) skein 6 (7) skeins

Pattern stitches for Grass-Basket Cropped Ruana Vest

DOUBLE EYELET RIBBING →

Worked flat as ribbing. All rows are charted here. Even-numbered rows are worked k2, *p5, k2, repeat from * across to last stitch. See page 146, step 3, for full instructions including selvedge stitches.

Repeat: 2 rows x 7 stitches (with 2 balancing stitches at end of row, as shown (*).

GRASS-BASKET PATTERN ↓

Worked flat on stockinette-stitch ground; purl even-numbered rows.

Repeat (inside box, rows 13 through 52): 40 rows x 42 stitches (stitches 2–43; stitch 1 is a balancing stitch that occurs only once at the edge of each row).

Rows 1 through 12 are set-up rows and are worked only once.

The bold numbers within the boxes help with stitch-counting in the open areas. The include only the stitches inside the horizontal repeat.

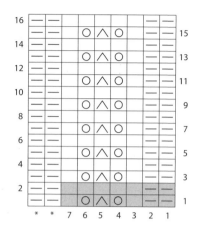

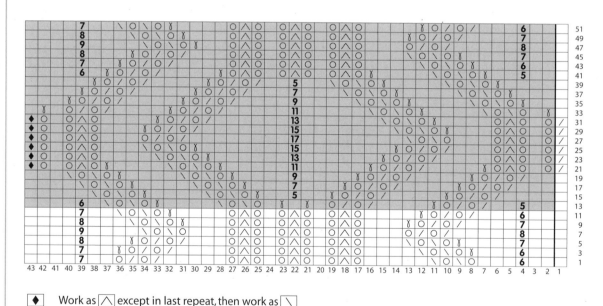

♦   Work as ∧ except in last repeat, then work as ＼

LEFT FRONT

1 Work only on left front stitches and continue to knit first and last stitches of every row for selvedge:

Work even in Grass-Basket pattern as established until left front measures same as right front to neck shaping.

2 Begin neck shaping: At neck edge, increase 1 stitch every right-side row 12 times, working increases in stockinette stitch.

End after a wrong-side row.

3 Work Garter Ridge pattern: Knit 6 rows.

Do not bind off. Cut yarn, leaving enough yarn attached to work three-needle bind-off to join shoulder.

SHOULDERS AND EDGING BANDS

1 Join each front shoulder to the corresponding number of stitches on the back shoulder with a three-needle bind-off. At back neckline, 15 stitches will remain open.

2 For the neckband, pick up 110 stitches along left front, knit the 15 live stitches across the back neck, pick up 110 stitches down right front.

Knit 5 rows (garter stitch).

Bind off very loosely. (See page 106 for a stretchy bind-off.)

3 For each armhole band, pick up 148 stitches evenly around armhole: Starting at underarm, pick up 74 stitches to shoulder seam, then 74 down the other side from shoulder seam to underarm.

Knit 5 rows (garter stitch).

Bind off loosely. Seam together ends of armhole bands at underarm.

FINISHING

Weave in ends. Press edging very lightly.

Wash and lay flat to dry. Do not stretch and pin to block or you will spoil the elasticity of the yarn, especially in the ribbing.

I found these buttons, made from caribou horn, in the gift shop of the University of Alaska Museum of the North. Many local yarn shops carry similar buttons made of reindeer antler or bone.

Double-Diamond Fingerless Gloves

The small diamond motif on these elegant fingerless gloves is perfect to decorate the back of your hand. I made these in black so the lace pattern would show off against my light skin and the gloves would match my favorite winter coat. Select a color that best suits your own skin tone and wardrobe.

Instructions

Note: *Make two gloves, adjusting for left and right hands in step 3.*

1 With smaller needles, cast on 42 (50) stitches. Place marker. Join and knit in the round.

2 Work 6 rounds of garter stitch, circular:

> *Round 1 and all odd rounds:* Knit.
>
> *Round 2 and all even rounds:* Purl.

3 Change to larger needles. Set up pattern:

> *Round 1 (right glove):* Pm, k21 (25), pm, k2 (4), pm, work Double Diamond chart, pm, k2 (4).
>
> *Round 1 (left glove):* Pm, k2 (4), pm, work Double Diamond chart, pm, k2 (4), pm, k21 (25).
>
> *Round 2:* Knit all stitches, slipping markers as you come to them.

Repeat rounds 1 and 2 until piece measures 5 inches (12.5 cm) from cast-on edge, or desired length to thumb opening.

4 Work thumb opening:

Work to end of round and turn.

Work back and forth, continuing in pattern as established, until thumb opening is desired length, approx. 1.5 inches (3.8 cm).

Re-join to work in the round and work even for 1 inch (2.5 cm).

The diamond pattern on the gloves was inspired by detailed trim found on fur parkas.

Photo © Clark James Mishler. Used by permission.

Double-Diamond Fingerless Gloves	
Sizes	Adult M (L)
Knitted measurements	7 (8) inches (18 [20.5] cm) circumference
Skill level	Intermediate
Gauge	6 stitches = 1 inch (2.5 cm) in stockinette stitch, blocked
Needles	2.75 mm / 2 U.S.—set of four or five double-pointed needles 3.25 mm / 3 U.S.—set of four or five double-pointed needles
Yarn	250 yards (229 m) lace-weight yarn
The yarn I used	Mini-Mills Lace Weight Qiviut, Black 100 percent qiviut 250 yards (229 m) in 1-ounce (28.5-g) skein 1 skein

5 Change to smaller needles. Work 6 rounds of garter stitch, circular, as in step 2.

Bind off loosely. Cut yarn.

FINISHING

Weave in ends.

Pattern stitch for Double-Diamond Fingerless Gloves

DOUBLE DIAMOND PATTERN

Worked on stockinette-stitch ground. When working in the round, knit even-numbered rounds. When working back and forth for thumb opening, purl even-numbered rows.

Repeat: 48 rounds x 17 stitches.

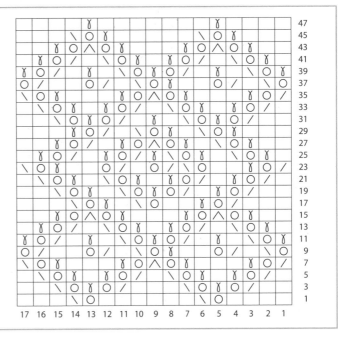

Easy Eyelet Gaiter

If you would like a nachaq, but aren't ready to invest in a project that takes three ounces of qiviut with an intricate lace pattern, this pared-down neck gaiter might be just right for you. Made with less than one ounce of qiviut-blend yarn and a simple eyelet rib stitch, it lets you practice lace knitting without a huge investment of time or money. This project also shows how you can use the simple ribbing and border stitches to design easy but beautiful garments.

Instructions

1 Cast on 114 stitches. Place marker and join to knit in the round.

2 Set up pattern:

Round 1: Work Easy Eyelet Ribbing chart around all stitches.

Round 2: (K3, p3) around.

Repeat rounds 1 and 2 until piece measures approx. 6.25 inches (16 cm) long.

Easy Eyelet Gaiter	
Sizes	One size
Knitted measurements	19 x 6.25 inches (48 x 16 cm)
Skill level	Easy
Gauge	Approx. 6 stitches = 1 inch (2.5 cm) in Easy Eyelet Ribbing stitch, as knitted
Needles	3.25 mm / 3 U.S.—circular, 16 inches (40 cm) or 20 inches (50 cm) long
Yarn	197 yards (180 m) lace-weight yarn
The yarn I used	Folknits Regular Lace Weight Qiviuq Blend, Light Natural 45 percent qiviuq, 45 percent wool, 10 percent silk 197 yards (180 m) in 25-g (.9-ounce) skein 1 skein

.3 Bind off loosely.

FINISHING

Weave in ends.

Wash and lay flat to dry. Do not stretch and pin to block or you will spoil the elasticity of the yarn and ribbing.

Pattern stitch for Easy Eyelet Gaiter

EASY EYELET RIBBING

Worked in the round; on even-numbered rounds, knit the knits and purl the purls (in effect, repeat k3, p3 around).

Repeat: 4 rows x 6 stitches.

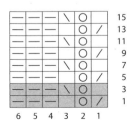

Hourglass Boa

This long, thin boa works equally well as a winter neck warmer or a summer scarf. A second version, knitted in hemp and shown on page 89, is an excellent example of how you can substitute less expensive yarns and still end up with beautiful results. The pattern shows up nicely in both yarns, yet the texture is completely different.

Instructions

1 Cast on 9 stitches, working loosely.

2 Pattern:

Row 1 (RS): Work Right Eyelet Edging chart, pm, work bottom triangle chart (one stitch in this row), pm, work Left Eyelet Edging chart.

Row 2 (WS): Slipping markers as you come to them across the row, k1, purl to last st, k1.

3 Continue pattern as established. Work bottom triangle chart (on page 155) once, body repeat chart (on page 156) 5 times, and top triangle chart (on page 157) once.

Pattern stitches for Hourglass Boa

EYELET EDGING #2

Worked flat on stockinette-stitch ground; purl even-numbered (wrong-side/WS) rows.

Knit right edging, body (hourglass) pattern, then left edging.

First and last stitches of each row are knitted, for a one-stitch garter-stitch edge on each side.

Repeat: 4 rows x 4 stitches (on each edge).

HOURGLASS PATTERN:

BOTTOM TRIANGLE

(KNIT FIRST)

Worked flat on stockinette-stitch ground; purl even-numbered (wrong-side/WS) rows.

Section: 52 rows.

Notes: This pattern is not outlined (no ktbl above yarn-overs). As usual, only right-side rows are charted. Be sure to use the make-one increase shown at the bottom of page 105.

Left eyelet edging:
Stitch 4 is edge stitch;
knit it on every row.

Right eyelet edging:
Stitch 1 is edge stitch;
knit it on every row.

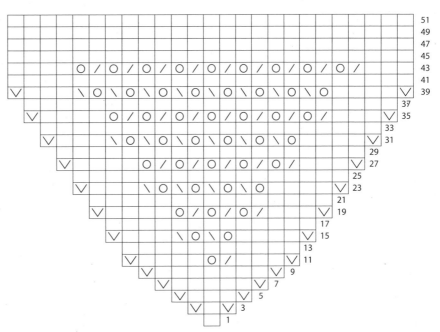

4 Bind off.

FINISHING

Weave in ends and block.

Add tassels on points. Make tassels in any way you choose, or use the basic instructions on page 157.

Hourglass Boa	
Sizes	One size
Knitted measurements	6 x 60 inches (15 x 152 cm), blocked
Skill level	Intermediate
Gauge	6 stitches = 1 inch (2.5 cm) in stockinette stitch, blocked
Needles	3.25 mm / 3 U.S.
Yarn	260 yards (238 m) sport-weight yarn
The yarn I used	Folknits Sport Weight Qiviuq, Natural 100 percent qiviuq 130 yards (119 m) in 25-g (.9-ounce) skein 2 skeins

Pattern stitches for Hourglass Boa

(continued)

HOURGLASS PATTERN: BODY

(KNIT SECOND)

Worked flat on stockinette-stitch ground; purl even-numbered (wrong-side/WS) rows.

Repeat (this entire chart): 74 rows x 25 stitches.

Note: This pattern is not outlined (no ktbl above yarn-overs). As usual, only right-side rows are charted.

The bold numbers within the boxes help with stitch-counting in the open areas. They include only the stitches inside the horizontal repeat.

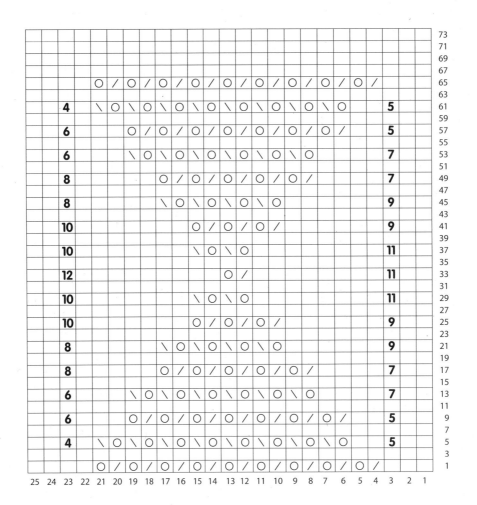

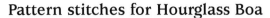

Pattern stitches for Hourglass Boa

(continued)

HOURGLASS PATTERN: TOP TRIANGLE
(KNIT LAST)

Worked flat on stockinette-stitch ground; purl even-numbered (wrong-side/WS) rows.

Section: 41 rows.

Note: This pattern is not outlined (no ktbl above yarn-overs). As usual, only right-side rows are charted.

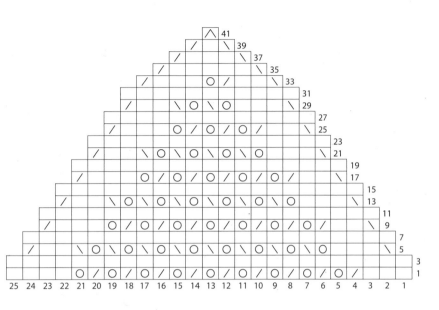

Basic tassel instructions

Cut a piece of cardboard 4 inches (10 cm) long.

Wrap yarn around the cardboard 25 times or until it's as full as you like.

Cut two pieces of yarn, one 6 inches (15 cm) long and the other 10 inches (25 cm) long. Thread the shorter piece of yarn between the cardboard and the yarn loops and use it to tie a secure knot around the loops where they cross one edge of the cardboard. Don't trim the tails of the knotted strand; you will use them to sew the tassel to the scarf.

Carefully slide the loops off the cardboard, keeping them orderly and aligned, with the tied knot at the top. Wrap the longer piece of yarn around the tassel about ½ inch (1.25 cm) from the top. Thread both tails of this strand through a needle and hide these ends in the center of the tassel.

Cut open the bottom loops of the tassel and trim the ends evenly. Sew the tassel in place using the loose ends of the first tying strand.

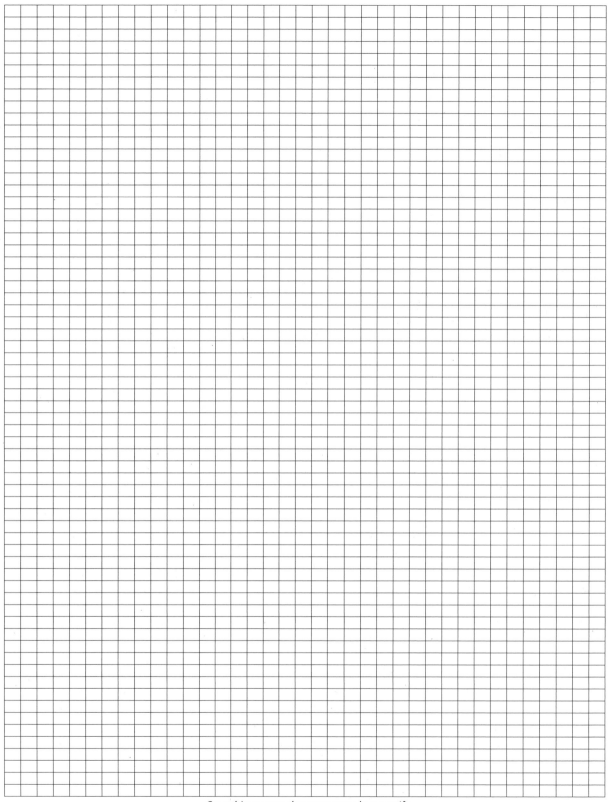

Copy this page to chart your own lace motifs.

Chapter 9

Designing your own projects

Designing your own lace projects is very rewarding. In this chapter you will find a library of lace pattern stitches to use in your own designs, tips on charting your own motifs, and generic instructions for several projects. Graph paper to copy for charting your own designs is on the opposite page.

Stitch library

The pattern stitches on the following pages, in addition to those used in the projects in Chapter 8, provide a starting point for designing your own knitted lace garments. Many of these stitch patterns are designed on right-side rows only. On the wrong-side rows, you need only knit or purl. I like to call these "rest rows," because you can relax and zip across the row. (This is not the case in all lace knitting, so always read charts carefully!)

Flat or circular; garter-stitch or stockinette ground

Most charts show odd-numbered, right-side (RS) rows only. Even-numbered rows are wrong-side (WS) rows.

- *All charts are given for flat knitting. For a stockinette-stitch background, purl wrong-side (WS) rows. If you prefer a garter-stitch background, knit the wrong-side (WS) rows. Some border and background stitches will not look right on a garter-stitch background, so make a test swatch to be sure you like the results.*
- *Notes in charts indicate any differences requred for circular knitting. For circular knitting, knit even-numbered rows for a stockinette-stitch background and purl them for a garter-stitch background.*

Legend

Symbol	Abbreviation	Description
(blank)		no stitch
.	k	knit on RS, purl on WS
−	p	purl on RS, knit on WS
O	yo	yarn-over
Ꝇ	ktbl	knit through back loop
/	k2tog	knit 2 together
\	k2tog-tbl	knit 2 together through back loops
∧	slip 1, k2tog, psso	slip 1, knit 2 together, pass slipped stitch over
∨	m1 or inc 1	make-1 increase or increase 1
⟈	slip 1, k1, yo, psso	slip 1, knit 1, yarn-over, pass slipped stitch over (both knitted stitch and yarn-over)
*	—	balancing stitch (for flat knitting, to center pattern)

Borders

Edgings for lace projects should lie flat and accent the main lace design. A variety of edgings can be used with lace. From simple seed stitch to lacy ribbings and scalloped edges, the borders illustrated here will inspire you to explore the possibilities for your own designs. Don't forget about garter stitch, the simplest border for knitted lace.

SEED STITCH

Both right-side and wrong-side rows shown.

Repeat: 2 rows x 2 stitches.

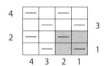

EYELET RIBBING

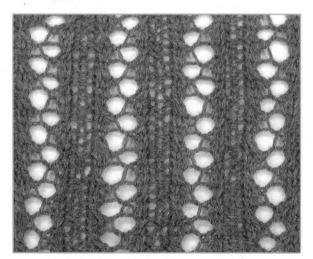

Both right-side and wrong-side rows shown. (On this pattern, do not knit through the back loop above yarn-overs.)

Repeat: 4 rows x 6 stitches (+ 2 stitches to balance on flat knitting [*]; omit balancing stitches for circular knitting).

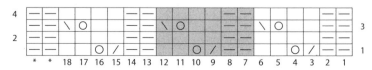

DOUBLE YARN-OVER COLUMN PATTERN

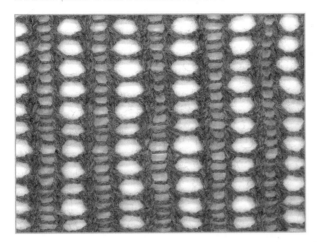

Only right-side rows shown. Purl wrong-side rows; however, on the wrong-side row you will purl and then knit into each double yarn-over (see page 103).

Repeat: 2 rows x 4 stitches.

\	O	O	/	\	O	O	/	\	O	O	/	7
\	O	O	/	\	O	O	/	\	O	O	/	5
\	O	O	/	\	O	O	/	\	O	O	/	3
\	O	O	/	\	O	O	/	\	O	O	/	1
12	11	10	9	8	7	6	5	4	3	2	1	

HERRINGBONE SCALLOPED EDGE

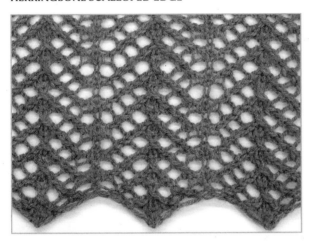

Only right-side rows shown. Purl wrong-side rows.

Repeat: 4 rows x 10 stitches (+ 1 stitch to balance on flat knitting [*]; omit balancing stitch for circular knitting).

	O	/	O	/			\	O	\	O		O	/	O	/			\	O	\	O		7
		O	/	O	∧	O	\	O					O	/	O	∧	O	\	O				5
	O	/	O	/			\	O	\	O		O	/	O	/			\	O	\	O		3
		O	/	O	∧	O	\	O					O	/	O	∧	O	\	O				1
*	20	19	18	17	16	15	14	13	12	11	10	9	8	7	6	5	4	3	2	1			

GARTER STITCH

Both right-side and wrong-side rows shown on chart. No swatch.

Repeat: 2 rows x 1 stitch.

Backgrounds

These simple stitch patterns work well for small projects and simple designs. They are excellent choices for new designers and new lace knitters, because the small pattern repeats are easy to memorize. They can also be used as border patterns on larger items, or combined in panel designs with elegant results (as in the Chevron Scarf on page 136).

For a variation on diagonal lines created by adding plain knit stitches between openwork lines, see the Wrist Warmers pattern on page 122.

SCATTERED EYELETS

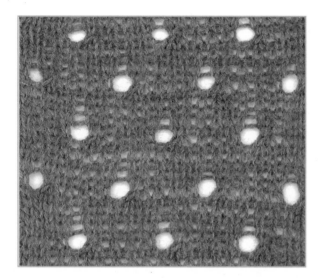

Only right-side rows shown. On this pattern, do not knit through the back loop above yarn-overs. While knitting through the back loop outlines the pattern, it also makes the yarn-over holes slightly smaller and I wanted to emphasize them here.

For circular knitting, simply work repeat as marked and knit even-numbered rounds.

For flat knitting, add balancing stitches [*] and purl even-numbered rows.

Repeat: 6 rows x 6 stitches.

FISHNET MESH

Only right-side rows shown. Best worked flat. Purl wrong-side rows.

Repeat: 4 rows x 2 stitches (+ 3 stitches to balance).

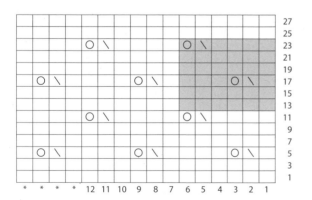

DIAGONAL LINES (LEFT-SLANTING)

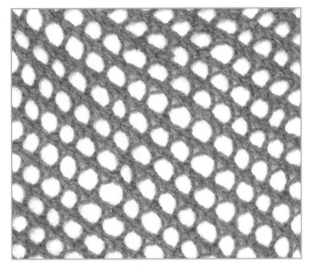

Only right-side rows shown on chart.

Stockinette-stitch ground.

For circular knitting, simply work repeat as marked and knit even-numbered rounds. Watch yarn-overs at beginnings of rounds 3 and 7 to make sure they stay on the correct side of the marker.

For flat knitting, add balancing stitches [*] and purl even-numbered rows.

Repeat: 4 rows x 2 stitches (+2 balancing stitches for flat knitting).

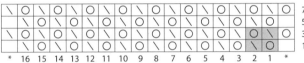

DIAGONAL LINES (RIGHT-SLANTING)

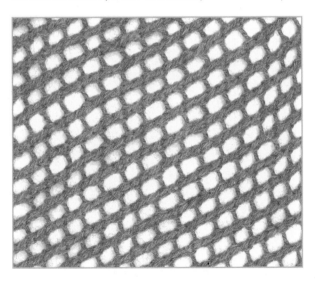

Only right-side rows shown on chart.

Stockinette-stitch ground.

For circular knitting, simply work repeat as marked and knit even-numbered rounds. Watch yarn-overs at beginnings of rounds 3 and 7 to make sure they stay on the correct side of the marker.

For flat knitting, add balancing stitches [*] and purl even-numbered rows.

Repeat: 4 rows x 2 stitches (+2 balancing stitches for flat knitting).

Panels

These larger stitch patterns are more detailed and complex than the previous patterns. Similar to the designs used by the Ooming-mak knitters, they require extra attention, but the results are spectacular. If you have experience knitting lace, you will find these patterns provide a challenge that will keep you from getting bored and that will make your knitting go quickly.

The wrong-side rows of these stitch patterns may be worked in garter or stockinette stitch, depending on your preference. The gauge will be different for each option, and the pattern will be subtler with a garter-stitch background. The charts are explained for, and the swatches are knitted with, a stockinette-stitch background.

Butterfly panel chart for flat knitting

Work balancing stitch [*] at beginning of row, then work shaded stitches for desired number of repeats, and end with balancing stitch at end of row [*]. Purl even-numbered rows.

♦   Work as △ except in last repeat, then work as ╲

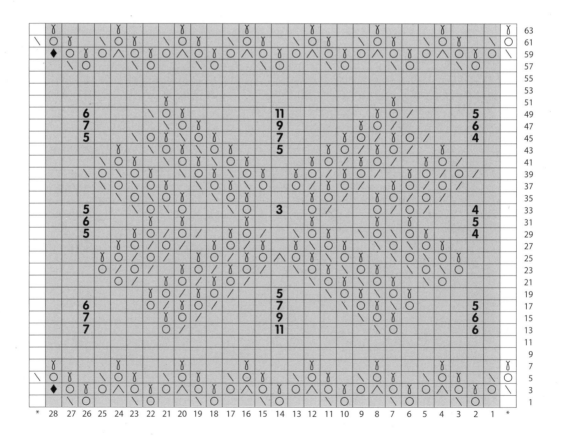

BUTTERFLY PANEL

Only right-side rows shown.

Repeat: 64 rows x 28 stitches (+2 balancing stitches for flat knitting).

Because the zigzag lines on this pattern are continuous with no plain knit stitches between repeats, this pattern starts and ends in slightly different positions for flat and circular knitting. This keeps the decreases from needing to cross the join between rounds.

Butterfly panel chart for circular knitting

For circular knitting, the entire chart is the repeat. Knit even-numbered rounds.

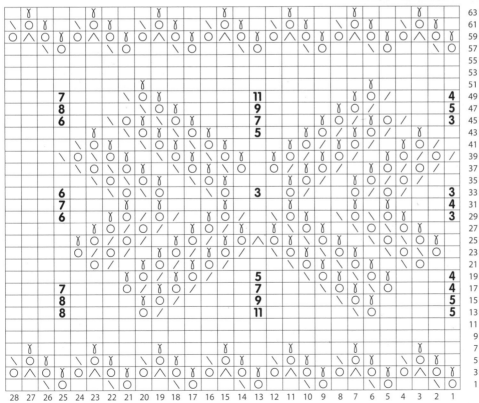

Diamond lattice parka-trim panel
(chart opposite top)

Church bells panel
(chart opposite bottom)

Snowflake panel
(chart on page 168)

DIAMOND LATTICE
PARKA-TRIM PANEL

Only right-side rows shown.

For flat knitting, purl even-numbered rows.

For circular knitting, knit even-numbered rounds.

Repeat: 78 rows x 25 stitches.

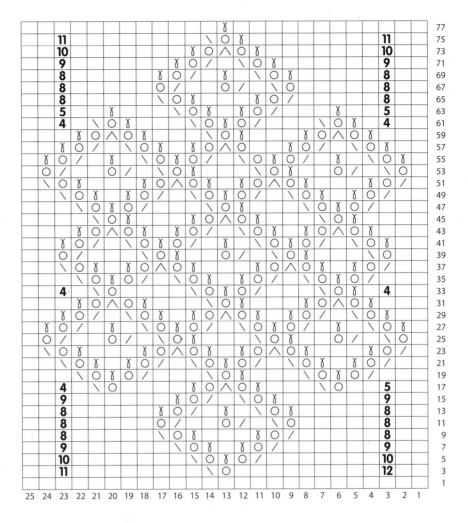

CHURCH BELLS PANEL

Both right-side and wrong-side rows shown. Worked on stockinette-stitch background.

Repeat: 14 rows x 20 stitches (plus 1 to balance for flat knitting [*]).

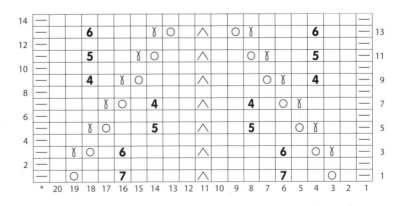

**SNOWFLAKE
PANEL**

Only right-side
rows shown.

For circular
knitting, knit even-
numbered rounds.

For flat knitting,
purl even-
numbered rows.

Repeat: 68 rows x
29 stitches.

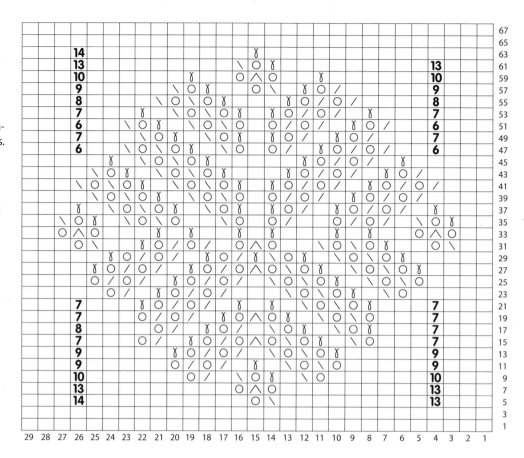

Yarn-over and decrease combinations

O /	**k2tog, yo** A right-leaning decrease almost always comes *before* a yo in a row.
\ O	**yo, k2tog-tbl** A left-leaning decrease almost always comes *after* a yo in a row.
\ O O /	**k2tog, yo 2x, k2tog-tbl** A double yarn-over is surrounded by decreases. On the next row (WS), purl into the first yo and knit into the second.
O ∧ O	**yo, slip 1, k2tog, psso, yo** Two yarn-overs are sometimes separated by a double decrease. This technique is used to form a double column of vertical holes, or the apex of a diamond.

Note: The charted symbols are read right to left.

Charting motifs

Charting your own lace pattern stitches is fairly simple, once you learn the basics. Your design tools are the yarn-over and decrease combinations shown in the chart on the previous page.

The primary design elements in lace motifs are the holes that "draw" the picture against a garter- or stockinette-stitch background. These holes are created by working yarn-overs on right-side rows.

1 When designing your own lace motif, first draw the yarn-overs on a blank chart. Unless you are intentionally charting a double yarn-over, be sure to leave at least one blank square between circles.

Each yarn-over must be accompanied by a decrease. The yarn-over creates a hole and at the same time adds one stitch. The accompanying decrease removes the extra stitch and at the same time may be used to draw an outline around the motif.

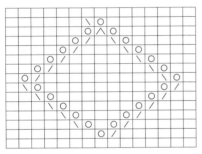

1

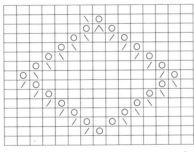

2b

2 The second step in designing your motif is deciding where to place the decreases.

When placing decreases before or after yarn-overs, you can either line up the decreases to outline the motif (2a) or stagger them to create a subtler design (2b).

3 The final step in charting your motif is adding the twisted stitches to complete the outline. Whenever you have a knit stitch on the right-side row above a yarn-over, knit that stitch in the back loop to twist it. This creates a clean edge that accentuates the design.

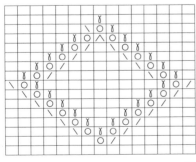

2a

3

Note: *Charts show right-side rows only.*

Basic pattern elements

Yarn-overs and decreases can be combined in many ways to create the building blocks for lace motifs.

Eyelets: Holes placed at regular intervals over a stockinette- or garter-stitch background create a subtle background pattern. Double eyelets are created by putting two yarn-overs next to each other.

| O \ | | / O |

Eyelets,
two variations

| O ⋀ O | | \ O O / |

Double eyelets,
two variations

Vertical lines: Stacking yarn-overs directly above each other for multiple right-side rows creates vertical lines. Stacking double yarn-overs creates a ladder.

Vertical lines,   *Ladder*
two variations

Horizontal lines: Alternating yarn-overs with decreases across a row creates a horizontal line.

Tips:
Charts show right-side rows only. Work on stockinette-stitch ground. For flat knitting purl even-numbered (wrong-side) rows. For circular knitting, knit even-numbered rounds.
* The first and last rows, marked with asterisks, show how to start or end a section of pattern. Just remember to pair yarn-overs with decreases, and vice versa.

Diagonal lines: Offsetting the yarn-overs by one stitch on each row creates a diagonal line.

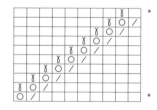

Diagonal line, left-slanting   *Diagonal line, right-slanting*

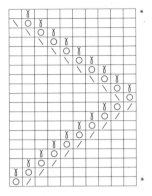

Vertical zigzag

Zigzags: Switching directions in the middle of a diagonal line creates a zigzag. Zigzags may be horizontal or vertical. A double decrease is required at the apex of a horizontal zigzag.

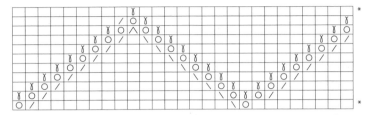

Horizontal zigzag

Diamonds: Once you know all of the basic lines, combining them to create diamonds is easy. In diamonds, the decreases are always below the yarn-overs. A double decrease is required at the apex of a diamond.

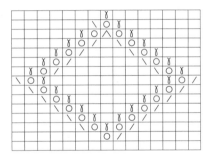

Curved lines: Working straight for one row where the line changes direction (arrow) creates a curve instead of a sharp point.

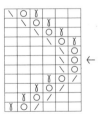

Curved background stitches: Moving the decreases away from the yarn-overs causes the background stitches to curve.

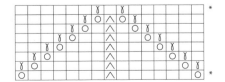

Pattern templates

Use these pattern templates as starting points for designing your own projects. (See Chapter 8 for step-by-step instructions for similar projects.)

Headband

This project can be knitted with any yarn from lace-weight to bulky. Select a pattern stitch with between 9 and 20 stitches for the center of the headband. Use garter stitch for borders. The width of the pattern stitch and the size of your yarn will determine the width of the headband.

1 Cast on 9 stitches.

2 Work in garter stitch and increase 1 stitch at the beginning of each row until you have the number of stitches in your pattern plus 6. End after working a wrong-side (WS) row.

3 Set up pattern with garter-stitch edges as follows:

K3, pm, work chart, pm, k3.

Continue working pattern as established, slipping markers when you come to them, until headband reaches from the center back of your neck, around your head, and just past your second ear.

4 Work in garter stitch and decrease 1 stitch at the beginning of each row until you have 9 stitches.

5 Bind off and sew ends together.

Scarf or shawl: End-to-end

This is the simplest of all patterns and is designed for lace-weight or sport-weight yarn. Use this pattern with a lace stitch that looks the same right side up and upside down, as in the North Star Scarf on page 126.

Work a gauge swatch first to see how wide one repeat of the main pattern stitch is. Use that measurement to decide how many times to repeat the pattern to achieve the desired width of the scarf or shawl.

For a scarf, cast on enough stitches for one or two repeats of the main pattern across the width. For a shawl, add additional pattern repeats to reach the desired width.

Headband

Scarf or shawl, end-to-end

1 Cast on the number of stitches required for the desired width. Round up or down to get the correct multiple for your border stitch and add extra stitches for side borders if desired. Use markers as needed to designate repeats.

2 Work border of choice.

3 Increase or decrease to the number of stitches in the panel repeats you have chosen, remembering to include stitches for side borders. Work patterns as established to desired length.

4 Increase or decrease as necessary and work border of choice.

5 Bind off loosely.

Scarf or shawl: End-to-center

This pattern is designed for lace-weight or sport-weight yarn. Use it when you choose a lace pattern that has an obvious direction—that looks best when "up" remains "up"—such as the Chevron Scarf on page 136.

Determine the number of stitches required for the width as in the end-to-end scarf, cast on, and work to one-half of the desired length. Repeat for the second half and graft the pieces together with Kitchener stitch.

1 Cast on the number of stitches required for the desired width. Round up or down to get the correct multiple for your border stitch and add extra stitches for side borders if desired.

2 Work border of choice.

3 Increase or decrease to the number of stitches in the panel repeats you have chosen, remembering to include stitches for side borders. Work patterns as established to one-half of desired length.

4 Do not bind off. Place the stitches on a holder.

5 Knit a second, identical piece.

6 Graft the two pieces together using Kitchener stitch, or, if you prefer, bind off very loosely using the three-needle bind-off. The three-needle option does not produce an invisible seam, but it creates a smooth join.

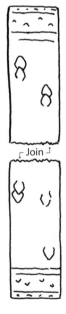

Scarf or shawl,
end-to-center

Möbius scarf

This pattern is designed for lace-weight or sport-weight yarn. It is like the end-to-end scarf but does not have any end-border stitches.

You begin the scarf with a provisional cast-on and do not bind off when you are finished. Instead, graft the two edges with a half-twist. Because a möbius is reversible, use garter stitch for the background (knit all wrong-side rows).

Determine the number of stitches required for the width as in the end-to-end scarf.

1 Cast on the number of stitches required for the desired width, adding extra stitches for side borders if desired.

2 Work patterns as established to desired length.

3 Make a half-twist in the scarf and graft the two ends together with Kitchener stitch.

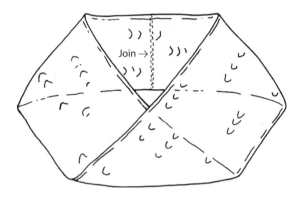

Möbius scarf

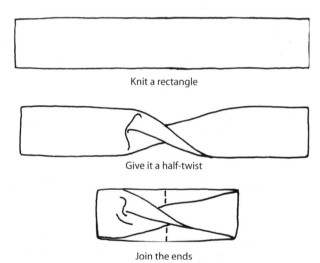

Knit a rectangle

Give it a half-twist

Join the ends

Nachaq hood

The pattern for this hood is designed for lace-weight or sport-weight yarn. It is similar to the möbius scarf pattern, but because it has no twist it can be knitted in the round. If you prefer not to purl, but like the texture of a stockinette-stitch background on your lace patterns, you will enjoy this pattern.

Determine the number of stitches required for width as in the end-to-end scarf.

Knit a tube

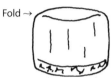

Fold →

Nachaq hood

1 Cast on the number of stitches required for the desired width. Round up or down to get the correct multiple for your border stitch. Join and knit in the round.

Note: *For an interesting variation, let the stitches twist once around the needle when you join. Because it creates a full twist, this is not a möbius, which has only one-half twist, yet it will result in a fascinating neck wrap. You will not need to graft the ends together.*

2 Work border of choice.

3 Increase or decrease to the number of stitches in the panel repeats you have chosen. Work pattern as established to desired length.

4 Increase or decrease as necessary and work border of choice.

5 Bind off loosely.

Wrist warmers

This pattern is designed for lace-weight or sport-weight yarn. Select a simple border stitch and you'll be able to whip out a pair of wrist warmers in a weekend.

Because they're small, you can combine your gauge swatch with the actual start of the project. Estimate the gauge based on the recommended gauge and needle size for your yarn. Cast on and begin knitting. If your gauge is off, you haven't wasted much time and you can easily start over on larger or smaller needles. However, if your gauge is correct, you have completed one wrist warmer instead of a swatch.

Wrist warmers

1 Cast on the number of stitches required for the desired width around the wrist. Round up or down to get the correct multiple for your pattern stitch. Join and knit in the round.

2 Work pattern stitch of choice until wrist warmers are desired length, approximately 4 inches (10 cm).

3 Bind off loosely.

Fingerless gloves

This pattern is designed for lace-weight or sport-weight yarn. These gloves are similar to the wrist warmers, but because they are longer and extend onto the hand you can use a more complicated stitch pattern and even add borders.

Left   *Right*

Fingerless gloves

Determine the number of stitches required for the width as for the wrist warmers.

1 Cast on the number of stitches required for the desired width around the wrist. Round up or down to get the correct multiple for your pattern stitch. Join and knit in the round.

2 Work border of choice.

3 Increase or decrease as necessary and work pattern stitch of choice until gloves are desired length to thumb opening, approximately 5 inches (12.5 cm).

4 To work thumb opening, work to end of round and turn. Work back and forth, continuing to follow chart, until thumb opening is desired length, approximately 1.5 inches (3.8 cm). Re-join to work in the round and work even for 1 inch.

(For a reminder on how to adapt and read charts for circular and flat knitting, see pages 96–97.)

5 Increase or decrease as necessary and work border of choice.

6 Bind off loosely.

Other projects

To use lace stitches in other projects, select a basic pattern that has little shaping. For a sweater or vest, a drop-shoulder or modified drop-shoulder design is easiest to adapt to lace. Shaping shoulders and armholes while maintaining a complicated lace pattern is quite challenging. (It can be done: I have several beautiful sweaters my grandmother made in this way.)

A lace poncho is also lovely, and fairly easy to design because ponchos can be made out of one or two rectangles that are sewn or grafted together.

For caps, select a watch cap, cloche, or basic tam pattern that has a fairly large straight panel on the sides of the hat. Use this area for a lace pattern. Most hats and caps are started at the brim and worked to the crown. Incorporating lace into the crown is quite difficult. Old-fashioned counterpanes and doilies were knitted circularly, starting in the center, with yarn-over increases arranged in interesting patterns. It would be a fun challenge to adapt some of these designs into lace-hat patterns. This is the technique I used in the North Star Tam on page 126.

Acknowledgments

Without the knitters of Oomingmak Musk Ox Producers' Co-operative and their dedication to making high-quality, hand-knit goods, this book would not exist. To the members who are knitting today, and to all of those who came before them, I give my deepest gratitude. In addition, to everyone who believed in the dream of domesticating the musk ox and using its luxurious fiber to create a cottage industry providing income to families in remote villages across Alaska, thank you!

Sigrun Robertson helped me plan my journey, welcomed me, took almost an entire day out from her busy schedule to talk about the history of the co-operative and relive memories of its early days, and later read my text with care to help it achieve the highest possible degree of accuracy.

Throughout my travels, I encountered generosity. The following people helped me immensely in my research. Sandy Belk-Ohs and Rick Moses at the Musk Ox Farm and Sandy Garbowski at LARS gave me private tours during the off-season, and Sandy Garbowski also read several sections of the manuscript to help me clarify details. Fran Degnan met with me in Unalakleet to talk about her experiences knitting for the co-op and her life in rural Alaska. Helen Howard took time to show me teaching materials from workshops with Dorothy Reade, and to reminisce about her early experiences at the co-op. She also, very helpfully, pointed out several holes in my research. At the University of Alaska Museum of the North in Fairbanks, Angela Linn and Brandy Jacobsen graciously allowed me to photograph items from the ethnology and mammal collections. Cathy Silbert, the interlibrary loan librarian at the Longmont Public Library was indispensable in my search for books about Alaska. I would have gone bankrupt buying books without her. Debbie O'Neill, Monika Bukor, and Joanne Conklin test-knitted several of the patterns and helped me refine the charts and instructions. To everyone else I met in my travels and studies, thank you!

I would also like to thank my editor, Deb Robson, for believing in my idea, for helping me clarify my vision to turn piles of research into a lively and interesting book, and for fixing all of my misplaced commas. Mayapriya Long of Bookwrights created a beautiful cover design that conveys the spirit of Oomingmak. Kathryn Banks copyedited, proofread, and indexed. Natalie Giboney of Freelance Permissions saved me untold hours tracking down and obtaining permission to use the historical photos in this book, and Rebekah Robson-May worked digital magic with all of the photos from many different sources to make sure everything looked as good as it possibly could. Gayle Ford provided essential drawings. My husband, Dominic Cotignola, went beyond the line of duty when he accompanied me in my travels across Alaska taking pictures and visiting museums, farms, knitting shops, and people—without getting even one chance to go fishing.

Sources

The availability of qiviut changes frequently. When I was working on Arctic Lace, I was able to obtain yarn for knitting and photos of fiber from only a few manufacturers. As we go to press, the companies listed below as sources for qiviut sell it as a raw material or in the form of finished items. Those who offer yarn supply high-quality materials that can be used for this book's projects with beautiful results.

Qiviut

Belfast Mini-Mills Ltd.
Yarn, roving, and knitted items
1820 Garfield Road, RR #1
Belfast, Prince Edward Island C0A 1A0 Canada
902–659–2202
www.minimills.net

Caryll Designs
Yarn and spinning fiber, with appreciation to Nancy Bender, founder of MOCO yarns
301 Sandy Creek Road / PO Box 30
Tendoy, ID 83468-0030
208-756-4702; 888-566-6812
www.carylldesigns.com

Folknits
Yarn, kits, and knitted items
2093 Second Avenue
Whitehorse, Yukon Y1A 1B5 Canada
867–668–7771
www.folknits.com

Jacques Cartier Clothier & Qiviuk Boutiques
Yarn, roving, and knitted and woven garments
131A Banff Avenue / PO Box 22
Banff, Alberta T1L 1A2 Canada
403–762–5445
www.qiviuk.com

Oomingmak executive director Sigrun Robertson packages a tunic.

Photo courtesy of Oomingmak Musk Ox Producers' Co-operative.

Large Animal Research Station (LARS)
Yarn and spinning fiber
Institute of Arctic Biology—UAF
PO Box 757000
Fairbanks, AK 99775-7000
907–474–7945
www.uaf.edu/lars/qiviut.html

Mountain Shadow Farm
Yarn, roving, and knitted items
60 Orr Road, Jericho, VT 05465
802–899–5164
www.mountainshadowfarm.com

Oomingmak Musk Ox Producers' Co-operative
Hand-knitted items, knitted cap kit
604 H Street, Anchorage, AK 99501
907–272–9225; 888–360–9665 (outside Alaska)
www.qiviut.com

Qiveut Collection
Hand-knitted items
PO Box 909, Palmer, AK 99645
907–745–5838; 800–478–5838
www.qiveut.com

Windy Valley Muskox
Yarn and spinning fiber
HC 04 Box 9220, Palmer, AK 99645
907–745–1005
www.windyvalleymuskox.com

Arnica Lykkegaard
Yarn and knitted shawls
Hobrovej 69
8830 Tjele, Denmark
+ 45 86 61 22 67
arnica.dk / (English: arnica.dk/index.php?adLinkFrom = google&language = uk)

Lace blocking wires

Halcyon Yarn
12 School Street, Bath, ME 04530
800-341-0282
www.halcyonyarn.com

HandWorks Northwest, LLC
PO Box 19322, Portland, OR 97219
www.HandWorksNW.com
A portion of the proceeds is donated to the Susan G. Komen Breast Cancer Foundation

KnitPicks
13118 NE 4th Street, Vancouver, WA 98684
800-574-1323
www.knitpicks.com

Glossary

akutuq   Eskimo ice cream made of cooked fat, meat, and berries.

angyaq   Large Aleutian skin boat often used for whaling and long-distance travel. Also a synonym for umiak.

Athabascan, Eyak, Tlingit, Haida and Tsimshian   Indian groups in Alaska. See Chapter 2 for more information.

boss   Bony area on male musk ox head where the horns connect in the center of the skull.

brown fat   Fat in the hump of musk oxen that provides energy during the winter when food is scarce.

Cup'ik   Eskimos of Nunivak Island. Closely related to the Yup'ik people of mainland Alaska.

enu   Subterranean family house made of wood or whalebone with a sod covering.

Eskimo ice cream   A traditional treat. Often made from seal oil, trout, and salmonberries. Sometimes made with shortening today.

Eskimos   A group of peoples living in the Arctic coastal regions of North America, parts of Greenland, and northeast Siberia. Includes Yup'ik, Cup'ik, Siberian Yup'ik, and Inupiat peoples of Alaska, and the Inuit of Canada and Greenland. See Chapter 2 for more information.

guard hair   Long, stiff outer coat of the musk ox.

honeybucket   Port-a-potty, often comprising a bucket with a carrying handle, toilet seat, and lid.

housewife   Bag to hold a sewing kit.

Iditarod   Annual dog sled race.

igloo or iglu   A house not usually made of ice in Alaska, but of sod covering a subterranean bone or wooden frame. Also may refer to a beaver dam.

INAR   Institute of Northern Agricultural Research, founded by John Teal to investigate and promote musk ox domestication.

Inuit and Inupiat   Canadian and Alaskan terms, respectively, for the aboriginal inhabitants of the North American Arctic from Bering Strait to East Greenland.

kashim   *See* **qassiq.**

kuspuk   A summer parka, now often made from brightly colored cotton fabric.

LARS   Robert G. White Large Animal Research Station.

mukluks   Boots.

musk ox, muskox, musk-ox   Common spellings. Plural is usually *oxen*.

nachaq   Hood.

Native Alaskans   Indigenous peoples of Alaska including Eskimos, Indians, and Aleuts.

niqipiaq   Native food prepared off the land. Often used to refer specifically to meat.

oomingmak   Musk ox, literally "the bearded one." Also, the name of the Musk Ox Producers' Co-operative.

Outsider   Any person who is not from Alaska.

Ovibos moschatus   Musk ox.

parka   Winter garment, made of fur, feathers, or waterproof fishskin or fish gut.

qassiq A community dwelling, often called the "men's house" because men spent their days here working and teaching boys. The entire community also used this house for celebrations and festivals. Also appears as **kashim, qasgiq.**

qayaq Kayak or canoe. A small skin-covered boat used for local travel and hunting small mammals.

qiviut, qiviuq, qiviuk, and so forth Musk ox down. May also refer to the down of birds. "Qiviut" is trademarked by Oomingmak Musk Ox Producers' Co-operative to refer to the products they sell made from musk ox down.

skin sewing Sewing clothing and other items from animal skins instead of woven or knitted fabric.

snow machine Snowmobile.

snow-go Snowmobile.

storyknife A bone or ivory knife used by young girls to illustrate stories in the snow or mud.

umiak Large Inupiat seafaring skin boat, sometimes with a sail. Often used for long-distance travel and whaling.

Unangax^ Aleuts. Native Alaskans of the Aleutian Islands and coastal areas of southwest Alaska.

village A town that was the location of a traditional Native Alaskan community.

Yup'ik Eskimos of the southwest coastal areas of Alaska and extreme northeastern Siberia.

Abbreviations

dp	double-pointed
k	knit
k2tog	knit 2 stitches together
m1	make-one increase
p	purl
pm	place a marker
RS	right-side, right side
psso	pass slipped stitch over
sl	slip
sm	slip the marker
st	stitch
sts	stitches
tbl	through back loop (twists stitch)
WS	wrong-side, wrong side
yo	yarn-over

Chart symbols

	no stitch (blank)
☐	knit (k) on right side, purl (p) on wrong side
⊟	purl (p) on right side, knit (k) on wrong side
Ⓞ	yarn-over (yo)
Ɣ	knit through back loop (ktbl)
╱	knit two together (k2tog)
╲	knit two together through back loops (k2tog-tbl)
∧	slip one, knit two together, pass slipped stitch over (slip 1, k2tog, psso)
∨	make one (M1)
⧖	slip 1, knit 1, yarn-over, pass slipped stitch over both knitted stitch and yarn-over (slip 1, k1, yo, psso)
*	balancing stitch for flat knitting; allows you to center pattern

Unless otherwise noted in instructions, only odd-numbered rows/rounds are shown in the charts. These are the rows/rounds on which the lace patterning is worked.

Unless otherwise noted in instructions, even-numbered rows/rounds are purled in flat knitting and knitted when working in the round, producing a stockinette-stitch ground for the lace.

Bibliography

As you've learned, I was obsessed with my quest to learn about the Oomingmak knitters, qiviut, and the lace-knitting tradition that comes from Alaska. This resource list catalogs the materials that I read during my research. The resources marked with asterisks (*) would make good initial follow-ups to *Arctic Lace,* although your personal interests could lead you to some of the other excellent, but more specialized, information that I found.

Books

Andrews, Susan B., and John Creed. *Authentic Alaska: Voices of Its Native Writers.* Lincoln, Nebraska: Bison Books, 1998.

Barker, James H. *Always Getting Ready: Upterrlainarluta: Yup'ik Subsistence in Southwest Alaska.* Seattle: University of Washington Press, 1993.

Bordhi, Cat. *A Treasury of Magical Knitting.* Friday Harbor, Washington: Passing Paws Press, 2004.

Bruchac, Joseph. *Our Stories Remember: American Indian History, Culture, and Values through Storytelling.* Golden, Colorado: Fulcrum, 2003.

Chisholm, Colin. *Through Yup'ik Eyes: An Adopted Son Explores the Landscape of Family.* Portland, Oregon: Alaska Northwest Books, 2000.

Degnan, Frances Ann. *Under the Arctic Sun: The Life and Times of Frank and Ada Degnan.* Unalakleet, Alaska: Cottonwood Bark, 1999.

Fagan, Brian M. *Ancient North America: The Archeology of a Continent.* 2nd ed. New York: Thames and Hudson, 1995.

Fienup-Riordan, Ann. *Eskimo Essays: Yup'ik Lives and How We See Them.* New Brunswick, New Jersey: Rutgers University Press, 1990.

——— . *The Real People and The Children of Thunder: The Yup'ik Eskimo Encounter with Moravian Missionaries John and Edith Kilbuck.* Norman: University of Oklahoma Press, 1991.

——— . *Yup'ik Eskimos as Described in the Travel Journals and Ethnographic Accounts of John and Edith Kilbuck Who Served with the Alaska Mission of the Moravian Church, 1885–1900.* Kingston, Ontario: Limestone Press, 1988.

——— , ed. *Where the Echo Began and Other Oral Traditions from Southwestern Alaska Recorded by Hans Himmelheber.* Translated by Kurt and Ester Vitt. Fairbanks, Alaska: University of Alaska Press, 2000.

Fitzhugh, William W., and Susan A. Kaplan. *Inua: Spirit World of the Bering Sea Eskimo.* Washington, D.C.: Smithsonian Institution Press for the National Museum of Natural History, 1982.

Gray, David R. *The Muskoxen of Polar Bear Pass.* Markham, Ontario: Fitzhenry and Whiteside, 1987.

Haycox, Stephen. *Alaska: An American Colony.* Seattle: University of Washington Press, 2002.

Healy, Carol, ed. *Muskox Management Report of Survey-Inventory Activities, 1 July 2000–30 June 2002.* Juneau: Alaska Department of Fish and Game, Division of Wildlife Conservation, 2003.

Hicks, Mary V., ed. *Muskox Management Report of Survey-Inventory Activities, 1 July 1998–30 June 2000.* Juneau: Alaska Department of Fish and Game, Division of Wildlife Conservation, 2001.

Hill, Kirkpatrick. *Minuk: Ashes in the Pathway.* Middleton, Wisconsin: Pleasant Company Press, 2002.

Hilscher, Herb. *The Heritage of Alaska.* Anchorage: National Bank of Alaska, 1971.

Himmelheber, Hans. *Eskimo Artists.* 1938. Reprint, Fairbanks: University of Alaska Press, 1993.

Jacobson, Steven A. *Yup'ik Eskimo Dictionary.* Fairbanks: Alaska Native Language Center, 1984.

Jans, Nick. *The Last Light Breaking: Living Among Alaska's Inupiat Eskimos.* Seattle: Alaska Northwest Books, 1993.

Keithahn, Edward L. *Eskimo Adventure: Another Journey into the Primitive.* New York: Bonanza Books, 1963.

Kremers, Carolyn. *Place of the Pretend People: Gifts from a Yup'ik Eskimo Village.* Seattle: Alaska Northwest Books, 1996.

Laraux, Sis. *Our Side of the River: A Biography of Growing Up and Living in Alaska on Our Side of the Kuskokwim River in the Village of Old Akiak.* Palmer, Alaska: Publication Consultants, 1994.

Lee, Molly. *Baleen Basketry of the North Alaskan Eskimo.* 1983. Reprint, Seattle: University of Washington Press, 1998.

* Lent, Peter C. *Muskoxen and Their Hunters: A History.* Norman: University of Oklahoma Press, 1999.

Lenz, Mary, and James H. Barker. *Bethel: The First 100 Years, 1885–1985.* Bethel, Alaska: City of Bethel Centennial History Project, 1985.

Lopez, Barry. *Arctic Dreams.* New York: Scribner, 1986.

Lord, Nancy. *Green Alaska: Dreams from the Far Coast.* Washington, D.C.: Counterpoint, 1999.

* Matthiessen, Peter. *Oomingmak: The Expedition to the Musk Ox Island in the Bering Sea.* New York: Hastings House, 1967.

McClanahan, Alexandra J. *A Reference in Time: A Native History Day by Day.* Anchorage: The CIRI Foundation, 2001.

Milepost. *The Alaska Wilderness Guide.* 8th edition. Augusta, Georgia: Morris Communications Corporation, 2001.

Million, Marsha, ed., and Anchorage Community College Toksook Bay Adult Education Class. *Stories from Toksook Bay.* Translated by Eliza Chanar. 1978. Reprint, Anchorage, Alaska: Circumpolar Press, n.d.

Movius, Phyllis Demuth, ed. *When the Geese Come: The Journals of a Moravian Missionary, Ella Mae Ervin Romig, 1898–1905, Southwest Alaska.* Fairbanks: University of Alaska Press, 1997.

Muir, John. *Travels in Alaska.* Boston: Houghton Mifflin, 1915.

Nelson, Edward W. *The Eskimo About Bering Strait.* 1899. Reprint, Washington, D.C.: Smithsonian Institution Press, 1983.

Netsvetov, I. E. *The Journals of Iakov Netsvetov: The Yukon Years, 1845–1863.* Edited by Richard A. Pierce. Translated with an introduction and supplementary material by Lydia T. Black. Kingston, Ontario: Limestone Press, 1984.

Niven, Jennifer. *Ada Blackjack: A True Story of Survival in the Arctic.* New York: Hyperion, 2003.

Oakes, Jill E., and Rick Riewe. *Our Boots: An Inuit Women's Art.* New York: Thames and Hudson, 1996.

Orr, Eliza Cingarkaq, Ben Orr, Victor Kanrilak Jr., and Andy Charlie Jr. *Ellangellemni . . . When I Became Aware. . . .* Fairbanks: Lower Kuskokwim School District and Alaska Native Language Center, 1997.

Oswalt, Wendell H. *Alaskan Eskimos.* Scranton, Pennsylvania: Chandler Publishing Company, 1967.

———. *Bashful No Longer: An Alaskan Eskimo Ethnohistory, 1778–1988.* Norman: University of Oklahoma Press, 1990.

———. *Mission of Change in Alaska: Eskimos and Moravians on the Kuskokwim.* San Marino, California: The Huntington Library, 1963.

Pedersen, Sverre, Terry L. Haynes, and Robert J. Wolfe. *Historic and Current Use of Musk Ox by North Slope Residents, with Specific Reference to Kaktovik, Alaska.* Technical Paper No. 206. Juneau: Alaska Department of Fish and Game, 1991.

Rau, Margaret. *Musk Oxen: Bearded Ones of the Arctic.* New York: Thomas Y. Crowell, 1976.

Ray, Dorothy Jean. *Aleut and Eskimo Art: Tradition and Innovation in South Alaska.* Seattle: University of Washington Press, 1981.

———. *The Eskimos of Bering Strait, 1650–1898.* 1976. Reprint, Seattle: University of Washington Press, 1991.

———. *A Legacy of Arctic Art.* Seattle: University of Washington Press, 1996.

* Reade, Dorothy. *25 Original Knitting Designs.* Eugene, Oregon: Dorothy Reade, 1968.

Richards, Eva Alvey. *Arctic Mood: A Narrative of Arctic Adventures.* Caldwell, Idaho: Caxton Printers, 1949.

* Sparks, Kathy. *Song of the Muskox.* Unionville, Indiana: The Hand Maiden, 1993.

Sturtevant, Willam C., general ed. David Damas, volume ed. *Handbook of North American Indians, Volume 5: Arctic.* Washington, D.C.: Smithsonian Institution, 1984.

Tennant, Edward A., and Joseph N. Bitar, eds. *Yup'ik Lore: Oral Traditions of an Eskimo People.* 1981. Reprint, Bethel, Alaska: Lower Kuskokwim School District, 1995.

Webster, Donald H., and Wilfried Zibell. *Iñupiat Eskimo Dictionary.* Fairbanks: Summer Institute of Linguistics, 1970.

Wilder, Edna. *Secrets of Eskimo Skin Sewing.* Fairbanks: University of Alaska Press, 1998.

Wohlforth, Charles. *The Whale and the Supercomputer: On the Northern Front of Climate Change.* New York: Farrar, Straus, and Giroux, 2004.

Zagoskin, Lavrentii Alekseevich. *Lieutenant Zagoskin's Travels in Russian America, 1842–1844: The First Ethnographic and Geographic Investigations in the Yukon and Kuskokwim Valleys of Alaska.* Edited and translated by Henry N. Michael. Toronto: University of Toronto Press, 1967.

Periodicals

Bergen, Werner von. "Musk-Ox Wool and Its Possibilities as a New Textile Fiber, part 1." *The Melliand* 3, no. 6 (September 1931): 472–474.

——. "Musk-Ox Wool and Its Possibilities as a New Textile Fiber, part 2." *The Melliand* 3, no. 7 (October 1931): 553–556.

——. "Musk-Ox Wool and Its Possibilities as a New Textile Fiber, part 3." *The Melliand* 3, no. 8 (November 1931): 646–648.

——. "Musk-Ox Wool and Its Possibilities as a New Textile Fiber, part 4." *The Melliand* 3, no. 9 (December 1931): 743–745.

——. "Musk-Ox Wool and Its Possibilities as a New Textile Fiber, part 5." *The Melliand* 3, no. 10 (January 1932): 844–846.

Bergman, Charles. "A Brave Return from the Brink for an Ice Age Relic." *Smithsonian* 16, no. 11 (February 1986): 68–77.

Berlo, Janet Catherine. "Oomingmak in Alaska: The Story of a Yup'ik Eskimo Knitting Co-op." *Inuit Art Quarterly* 10, no. 1 (Spring 1995): 17–21.

——. "Oomingmak: Knitting Vision into Reality." *PieceWork* 4, no. 1 (January/February 1996): 50–53.

* Chambers, Wendy. "Qiviuq." *Spin-Off* 17, no. 2 (Summer 1993): 48–52.

——. "A Qiviut Cap to Knit." *PieceWork* 4, no. 1 (January/February 1996): 54–55.

Cornwall, E. Marguerite. "Some Hints on Spinning Musk Ox Wool." *Spin-Off* 7, no. 1 (March 1983): 20–22.

Cortright, Linda N. "Alaskan Pastures." *Wild Fibers* 1, no. 1 (Winter 2004): 12–17.

DeVaughn, Melissa. "Beasts of No Burden: Musk Oxen's Qiviut Keeps Rural Knitting Program Alive." *Alaska* 69, no. 9 (November 2003): 36–41.

Drew, Lisa W. "Meet the Neighbors: As Their Numbers Continue to Increase in Alaska, Muskoxen Are Turning up in Some Unexpected Places." *National Wildlife* 40, no. 3 (April/May 2002). Located online at < http://www.findarticles.com/p/articles/mi_m1169/is_2002_April-May/ai_89436232 > (July 15, 2005).

Druchunas, Donna. "Exotic Fibers for Knitters." *Interweave Knits* 8, no. 3 (Fall 2003): 42–45.

Franz, Bonnie. "Yarn Review: Qiviut." *Stranded Newsletter* 2, no. 4 (Autumn 2004): 13.

Griffiths, Helen M. "Arctic Handknitted: One Hundred Percent Qiviut." *Handweaver & Craftsman* 22, no. 2 (Spring 1971): 6–8, 38–39.

——. "Qiviut From the Musk Ox." *Handweaver and Craftsman* 18, no. 3 (Summer 1967): 5–6, 36–27.

Hoogendorn-Alowa, Lee Ann. "The Story of Eskimo Ice Cream." *Kaŋiqsirugut News* no. 49 (June/August 2002): 20.

Howard, Helen Griffiths "The Musk Ox." *Spin-Off* 7, no. 1 (Spring 1983): 16–19.

Hudson, Marjorie, and Kathy Sparks. "Arctic Adventures with Qiviut." *Spin-Off* 11, no. 3 (Fall 1987): 47–49.

* Irwin, Bobbie. "Domesticating the Musk Ox." *Spin-Off* 17, no. 2 (Summer 1993): 56–57.

* ——. "Montana Qiviut." *Spin-Off* 17, no. 2 (Summer 1993): 58–60.

* ——. "That Curious 'Q' Word." *Spin-Off* 17, no. 2 (Summer 1993): 52–53.

Kershaw, Sarah. "Modern Life Invades Insular Eskimo Tribe." *Denver Post,* Thursday, September 23, 2004: 25A.

Ketchum, Linda. "In Search of the Golden Fleece." *Alaska Magazine* (August 1989): 20–23.

Leask, Linda, Mary Killorin, and Stephanie Martin. "Trends in Alaska's People and Economy." Paper for the Alaska 20/20 Partnership Bringing Alaskans Together to Chart Our Future by the Institute of Social and Economic Research, University of Alaska Anchorage and the Alaska Humanities Forum. October 2001.

MacNulty, Shirley. "Qiviut Yarns." *INKnitters* 1, no. 3 (Winter 2001): 12–14.

Nelson, Elizabeth. "The Ultimate Ungulate." *Wild Fibers* 1, no. 1 (Winter 2004): 24–27.

* Olthuis, Diane. "Spinning Musk Ox Hair." *Spin-Off* 17, no. 2 (Summer 1993): 53–54.

Name note: Helen M. Griffiths, Helen Griffiths Howard, and Helen M. Howard are the same person.

Reed, Fran. "Summary of Wool Bureau Report on Musk Ox Fiber." *Spin-Off* 7, no. 1 (Spring 1983): 42.

Rennick, Penny, ed. "Inupiaq and Yupik People of Alaska." Special issue, *Alaska Geographic* 28, no. 3 (2001).

———. "Moose, Caribou and Muskox." Special issue, *Alaska Geographic* 23, no. 4 (1997).

Rosing, Norbert. "Muskoxen." *National Geographic* 201, no. 4 (April 2002): 76–89.

Rowell, J. E., C. J. Lupton, M. A. Robertson, F. A. Pfeiffer, J. A. Nagy, and R. G. White. "Fiber Characteristics of Qiviut and Guard Hair from Wild Muskoxen (*Ovibos moschatus*)." *Journal of Animal Science* 79 (2001): 1670–1674.

* Sparks, Kathy. "Dorothy Reade: A Woman Ahead of Her Time." *Spin-Off* 17, no. 2 (Summer 1993): 61–62.

Struzik, Ed. "And Then There Were 84,000: The Return of Musk-Oxen to Canada's Banks Island in Recent Decades Is Just One Chapter of a Beguiling Arctic Mystery." *International Wildlife* 30, no. 1 (January/February 2000): 28–35.

Tarrant, Bert. "Alaskan Qiviut is World's Rarest Textile Prize." *Alaska Journal of Commerce and Pacific Rim Reporter,* February 12, 1979:10–12.

* Teal, John J., Jr. "Domesticating the Wild and Woolly Musk Ox." *National Geographic* 169, no. 6 (June 1970): 862–879.

———. "Musk Ox in Rut." *Polar Notes* no. 1 (November 1959): 65–71.

Tetpon, John. "Changes Needed to Better Native Lives." *Anchorage Daily News,* Thursday, April 15, 2004, B-4.

Tizon, Tomas Alex. "Alaskan Villages in Hot Water: Rising Temperatures Melt Ice Barriers, Imperil Communities." *Los Angeles Times,* Sunday, November 7, 2004.

* von Ammon, Helen. "Guard Hair to Garment." *Spin-Off* 17, no. 2 (Summer 1993): 54–55.

Walter, Patty. "On the Wing with Bishop Kettler: Part II." *The Alaskan Shepherd* 41, no. 2 (March 2003): 1–6.

Wilkinson, Paul F. "The Length and Diameter of the Coat Fibres of the Musk Ox." *Journal of Zoology* 177 (1975): 363–375.

———. "Wool Shedding in Musk Oxen." *Biological Journal of the Linnean Society* 6, no. 2 (June 1974): 127–141.

Wons, Joanna. "Musk Ox Madness." *Spin-Off* 17, no. 2 (Summer 1993): 60–61.

The Internet

aboriginaltimes. "Nunavut: Flexing Its Economic Muscle." aboriginaltimes, November 2003. < http://www.aboriginaltimes.com/economic-development/nunavut-economy/view > (5/25/2005).

* Alaska Native Heritage Center. *Alaska Native Heritage Center.* < http://alaskanative.net/ > (5/27/2005).

Alaska, State of: Department of Commerce, Community, and Economic Development. *Alaska Community Database Online.* < http://www.commerce.state.ak.us/dca/commdb/CF_CIS.cfm > (6/8/2006).

———. *Alaska Photo Library.* < http://www.commerce.state.ak.us/apl/home.cfm > (5/25/2005).

Alaska's Virtual Library and Digital Archives. *Alaska's Digital Archive.* < http://vilda.alaska.edu/ > (5/25/2005).

Alaska Travel Industry Association. *Travel Alaska.* < http://travelalaska.com/ > (5/24/2005).

Arctic Circle. *Arctic Circle History and Culture.* < http://arcticcircle.uconn.edu/HistoryCulture/ > (5/25/2005).

Atkinson, Frank H., "The Papers of Frank H. Atkinson at Dartmouth College." *Digital Library at Dartmouth.* < http://ead.dartmouth.edu/html/stem6.html > (5/25/2005).

BBC News. "Alaskans Face the Thaw." *BBC News: World: Americas,* Wednesday, November 15, 2000. < http://news.bbc.co.uk/1/hi/world/americas/1024585.stm > (5/25/2005).

Becker, Sylvia. "Qiviut (or Qiviuk): Information for Knitters and Spinners." *FiberLink* and *The Fiber Gypsy.* < http://www.fibergypsy.com/fibers/qiviut.shtml > (5/25/2005).

Beckett, Elizabeth, and Sarah Teel. "Eskimo Women." *ThinkQuest Library.* < http://library.thinkquest.org/11313/Early_History/Native_Alaskans/eskimo.html > (5/25/2005).

Beckett, Joel. "Muskox (*Ovibos moschatus*)." *"Animals of the Arctic." ThinkQuest Library.* < http://library.thinkquest.org/3500/muskox.html > (5/25/2005).

Bering Strait School District. "The History and Importance of Custom-fit Traditional Fur Clothing." *The Custom-Designed Traditional Fur Clothing of Wilma Osborne.* < http://www.bssd.org/eskimo_art/specia11.html > (5/25/2005).

————. *Yupik Web Site.* < http://www.bssd.org/sites/gam/yupik/yupik.htm > (6/6/2002; not an active site as of 7/15/2005).

Brant, Tataboline. "Musk Oxen May Finally Pay: Project Aims to Boost Diet, Qiviut Yield." *Anchorage Press* 8, no. 31 (August 5–11, 1999). < http://anchoragepress.com/archives/document4201.html > (5/27/2005).

Brown, Marciella, September Laakso, Anne McBeth, and Tara Maginnis. "Alaska Native Traditional Dress Bibliography." *The Costumer's Manifesto.* < http://www.costumes.org/ETHNIC/1PAGES/AKBIBLIO.HTM > (5/25/2005).

Brown, Paul. "Global Warming Is Killing Us Too, Say Inuit." *The Guardian,* Thursday December 11, 2003. < http://www.guardian.co.uk/international/story/0,3604,1104241,00.html > (5/25/2005).

Catholic Bishop of Northern Alaska. "Tununak— Saint Joseph" *Diocese of Fairbanks Official Web Site.* < http://www.cbna.info/churches/tununak.html > (5/25/2005).

Cooper, Ashley, Chris Ayres, and Mark Henderson. "Inuit Start to Feel the Heat in a World Warming Up." *Times Online,* November 17, 2004. < http://www.timesonline.co.uk/article/0,,3-1361816,00.html > (5/25/2005).

Edwards, Steve. "Savvy Shopping in Anchorage: Musk Ox Products Keep Buyers Warm." *Anchorage Daily News.* < http://www.alaskaonline.com/places/cities/anchorage/story/4485200p-4475508c.html > (5/27/2005).

Explore North. "Musk Ox Links." *Explore North.* < http://www.explorenorth.com/library/weekly/aa020101b.htm > (5/25/2005).

Garr, Robin. "Oomingmak Musk Ox Cooperative." *@grass-roots.org.* < http://www.grass-roots.org/usa/ooming.shtml > (5/25/2005).

Goldberg, Donald. "Climate Change and Arctic Impacts" *Center for International Environmental Law.* < http://ciel.org/Climate/Climate_Arctic.html > (5/25/2005).

Government of the Northwest Territories. "Muskox in the NWT." *NWT Wildlife and Fisheries—NWT Wildlife Species—Muskox.* < http://www.nwtwildlife.rwed.gov.nt.ca/NWTwildlife/muskox/muskoxtop.htm > (5/26/2005).

Gray, David R. "Muskox." *Hinterland's Who's Who.* < http://www.hww.ca/hww2p.asp?id = 95&cid = 8 > (5/25/2005).

Greenland National Tourist Board. *Greenland Guide Index.* < www.greenland-guide.gl/ > (5/25/2005).

Greenpeace. "Climate Change and Arctic Wildlife." *greenpeace.org,* February 2000. < http://archive.greenpeace.org/climate/arctic99/html/content/factsheets/arcticwildlife.html > (5/25/2005).

Hamilton, Lawrence C., and Carole L. Seyfrit. "Female Flight? Gender Balance and Outmigration by Native Alaskan Villagers." *Circumpolar Health,* 1993. < http://pubpages.unh.edu/ ~ lch/female_flight.pdf > (5/25/2005).

Heidenreich, Conrad E., Daniel Francis, Michelle Guitard, and Olaf Janzen. "Henry Kelsey: The Young Adventurer." *Pathfinders & Passageways: The Exploration of Canada.* < http://www.collectionscanada.ca/explorers/h24–1510-e.html > (5/25/2005).

Hill, Miriam. "Kugluktuk HTA Spins Dreams of Musk Ox Mill." *Nunatsiaq News,* January 25, 2002. < http://www.nunatsiaq.com/archives/nunavut020125/news/nunavut/20125_4.html > (5/25/2005).

Hills, Mark. "Wild Arctic Muskox Harvest on Banks Island Brings Employment to the Inuit of the North." *Hills Foods Ltd.,* December 1997. < http://hillsfoods.com/article1.html > (5/25/2005).

Huffman, Brent. "*Ovibos moschatus:* Musk Ox. An Ultimate Ungulate Fact Sheet." *The Ultimate Ungulate Page.* < http://www.ultimateungulate.com/Artiodactyla/Ovibos_moschatus.html > (5/25/2005).

Iditarod Trail Sled Dog Race. *Official Site of the Last Great Race.* < http://www.iditarod.com/background.html > (5/25/2005).

inAlaska.com. "Musk ox." *Wildlife.* < http://www.inalaska.com/alaska/wildlife/muskox.html > (5/25/2005).

Institute of Social and Economic Research, University of Alaska Anchorage. *Alaskool: Online Materials about Alaska Native History, Education, Languages, and Cultures.* < http://www.alaskool.org/ > (5/25/2005).

Karg, Pamela J. "Fingers and Needles: Alaskan Co-Op Turns Cashmere-Soft Musk Ox Wool into Hard Cash." *Rural Cooperatives Magazine,* March/April 2000. < http://www.rurdev.usda.gov/rbs/pub/mar00/needles.htm > (7/10/2006).

Kennedy, Barbara K., and Leta A. Krumrine. "Large-Scale Climate Change Linked to Simultaneous Population Fluctuations in Arctic Mammals." *Penn State Eberly College of Science.* < http://science.psu.edu/alert/Post11–2002.htm > (10/5/2004).

Krause, Hans. "Mammoth Fauna 3: The Muskox." *Hans Krause's Research Reports.* < http://hanskrause.de/HKHPE/index%20HKHPE%2016%2000.htm > (11/26/2004).

———. "Mammoth Fauna 4: The Muskox." *Hans Krause's Research Reports.* < http://hanskrause.de/HKHPE/index%20HKHPE%2017%2000.htm > (11/26/2004).

Kremers, Carolyn. "How Tununak Came to Me" (excerpt). *Creative Nonfiction* 1. < http://www.creativenonfiction.org/thejournal/articles/issue01/01kremers_howtununak.htm > (5/25/2005).

* Large Animal Research Station. *Large Animal Research Station Home Page* < http://www.uaf.edu/lars/ > (5/27/2005).

Lawler, James. "Return of the Muskox to Gates of the Arctic." *Natural Resource Year in Review—2000,* National Park Service, U.S. Department of the Interior, May 2000. < http://www2.nature.nps.gov/YearInReview/yir2000/pages/02_nps_science/02_04_lawler.html > (5/25/2005).

Lawrence, Raymond. "Kitikmeot Foods Ltd. and Kitikmeot Hunters and Trappers Association: Muskox Makes for Culinary Treat, and More." *Indian and Northern Affairs Canada.* < http://www.ainc-inac.gc.ca/nr/ecd/ssd/ma04_e.html > (11/19/2004).

Lewis, Carol E. "Musk Ox: An Historical Industry Looks Toward the Future." *AgroBorealis* 32, no. 1 (Spring/Summer 2000): 30–32. < http://nrm.salrm.uaf.edu/afes/pubs/agr02000.pdf > (5/25/2005).

Lincoln, Greg. "Tuqsuk–Toksook Bay: How Our Village Came to Be." *Online Toksook Bay!,* Sept. 14, 1998. < http://members.aol.com/klincoln45/t4.htm > (5/25/2005).

Macleod, Alan. "Local Woman Supplies Rare Muskox Wool." < http://www.yukonweb.com/community/yukon-news/1995/sept6.htmld > (5/22/2002; not an active site as of 7/15/2005).

Manitoba Museum of Man and Nature. "Inuit Cultures: Arctic Region." *Hudson's Bay Company Digital Collection.* < http://collections.ic.gc.ca/hbc/catex1c1.htm > (5/25/2005).

Mazuri. "Mazuri Musk Ox Diet." < http://www.mazuri.com/5z54.htm > (5/25/2005).

McBride, Rhonda. "Lone Eagle Flies Again: III: The Ways of Old." *Qayanek: Keeping Yupik Tradition Alive.* Reprint from KTUU-TV, Anchorage, Alaska, December 1999. < http://www.qayanek.com/eagle99/eagle3.html > (5/25/2005).

McConnel, Caryll. "MOCO Yarns: Qiviut Luxuriously Soft and Warm." *Caryll Designs.* < http://carylldesigns.com/MOCO_qiviut.htm > (5/25/2005).

Murphy, Kim. "Global Warming Could Put Alaskan Village Underwater." *Asheville Global Report,* No. 130, July 12–18, 2001. < http://www.agrnews.org/issues/130/environment.html > (5/25/2005).

* Musk Ox Farm. "Welcome to the Musk Ox Farm!" < http://www.muskoxfarm.org/ > (5/27/2005).

Nash, John, and Dianne Nash. *Windy Valley Muskox Home Page.* < http://www.windyvalleymuskox.com > (9/30/2004).

National Wild and Scenic River System. *Wild and Scenic Rivers by State (AK).* < http://www.nps.gov/rivers/wildriverslist.html#ak > (5/25/2005).

Nuniwarmiut Piciryarata Tamaryalkuti. *Nuniwarmiut Piciryarata Tamaryalkuti (Nunivak Cultural Programs).* < http://www.nunivak.org/index.html > (5/25/2005).

* Oomingmak Musk-ox Producers' Co-operative. *Oomingmak Musk-ox Producers' Cooperative Web Site.* < http://www.qiviut.com > (7/17/2005).

Ounalashka Corporation. "The Aleutian World War II National Historic Area." < http://www.ounalashka.com/Aleutian%20WWII%20National%20Historic%20Area.htm > (5/25/2005).

Pacific and Yukon Region, Environment Canada. "Column 247. Sturdy Muskox Thriving." *Your Yukon.* < http://www.taiga.net/yourYukon/c01247.html > (5/25/2005).

Polar Continental Shelf Project, National Resources Canada. "Productivity of Musk Ox in Commercially Harvested Areas of Banks Island." *What We Do.* < http://polar.nrcan.gc.ca/proj/1999/productivity_e.php > (7/15/2005).

Presbytery of the Yukon (Presbyterian Church U.S.A.). *The Yukon Presbyterian: An Unauthorized Biography.* < http://yukonpresbytery.com/YukonPresbytery/FrontMatter/contents.htm > (5/25/2005).

Reyhner, John. "American Indians Out of School: A Review of Shool-based Causes and Solutions." *Journal of American Indian Education* 31, no. 2 (January 1992). < http://jaie.asu.edu/v31/V31S3ind.htm > (5/25/2005).

Reynolds, Brad. "Fishing in Toksook Bay." *Company Magazine,* 2003. < http://www.companymagazine.org/v203/fishing.htm > (5/25/2005).

Rinear, Jeanne Ostnes, and Eleanor Ostnes Vistaunet. "Marshall, Fortuna Ledge and the Mining of Willow Creek." *The Community History Project.* < http://yukonalaska.com/communities/marsha111.html > (5/25/2005).

Robertson, Morgan. "Research Boosts Qiviut Production." *Arctic Science Journeys.* Radio script, 1999. < http://www.uaf.edu/seagrant/NewsMedia/99ASJ/10.29.99_Qiviut.html > (5/25/2005).

Rosen, Yereth. "Climate Changes Spur Plan for Alaska Village Move." For Reuters News Service, published on Planet Ark web site, June 10, 2005. < http://www.planetark.com/dailynewsstory.cfm/newsid/31200/news.htm > (6/19/2006).

Rozell, Ned. "The Muskox Odyssey: From Greenland to Alaska, via New Jersey. Article #1548." *Alaska Science Forum,* June 28, 2001. < http://gi.alaska.edu/ScienceForum/ASF15/1548.html > (5/25/2005).

Schneider, Doug, "Alaska Feels the Heat." *Arctic Science Journeys.* Radio script, 2001. < http://www.uaf.edu/seagrant/NewsMedia/01ASJ/06.08.01Alaska-heat.html > (5/25/2005).

———. "Musk Ox Farm." *Arctic Science Journeys.* Radio script, 1998. < http://www.uaf.edu/seagrant/NewsMedia/98ASJ/06.04.98_MuskOx.html > (5/25/2005).

SERRC—Alaska's Educational Resource Center. "Culturally Integrated Unit II. Shelters." *Answer Camp Curriculum.* < http://www.serrc.org/sites/answercamp/Curriculum/shelters.pdf > (5/25/2005).

Smetzer, Mary Beth. "Qiviut Yarn Knitters in Remote Villages Make Extra Cash." *Kenai Peninsula Online,* November 28, 2000. < http://peninsulaclarion.com/stories/112800/ala_112800ala0020001.shtml > (5/27/2005).

Smith, Tim. "Muskox." *Alaska Department of Fish and Game Wildlife Notebook Series: Muskox.* < http://www.adfg.state.ak.us/pubs/notebook/biggame/muskoxen.php > (7/15/2005).

Smithsonian National Museum of Natural History. *Arctic Studies Center.* < http://www.mnh2.si.edu/arctic/index.html > (5/25/2005).

Smythe, Charles W. "Eskimo (Yupik/Inupiat/Inuit)." *Encyclopedia of North American Indians. Houghton Mifflin.* < http://college.hmco.com/history/readerscomp/naind/html/na_011300_eskimo.htm > (5/25/2005).

Teal, John J., Jr. "The Papers of John J. Teal in the Dartmouth College Library." *Digital Library at Dartmouth.* < http://ead.dartmouth.edu/html/stem176.html > (5/25/2005).

Tennison, Rosalie I. "Qiviuq: Down of the North." *artloft2000.com: creativity is the key / Fibre North* 1, no. 1. < http://www.artloft2000.com/Qiviuq.htm > (5/30/2002; not an active site as of 7/15/2005).

U.S. Army Center of Military History. "Aleutian Islands." < http://www.army.mil/cmh-pg/brochures/aleut/aleut.htm > (5/25/2005).

U.S. Department of Interior, Bureau of Land Management. "Unalakleet National Wild River." < http://www.ak.blm.gov/ado/unk/unksetng.html > (11/21/2004; site under construction as of 7/15/2005).

U.S. Fish and Wildlife Service. "Muskox (*Ovibos moschatus*)." *Fish and Wildlife Species Home Page,* March 1995. < http://www.fws.gov/species/species_accounts/bio_musk.html > (7/18/2005).

U.S. National Parks Service. *Aleutian Natural History.* < http://www.nps.gov/aleu/AleutianNaturalHistory.htm > (5/25/2005).

———. "Aleutian World War II National Historic Area." < http://www.nps.gov/aleu/home.htm > (5/25/2005).

University of Alaska Anchorage. *LitSite Alaska.* < http://litsite.alaska.edu/ > (5/25/2005).

University of Alaska Anchorage Archives. "Unalakleet Evangelical Covenant Church. Records; 1888–1981." One reel, microfilm. < http://www.lib.uaa.alaska.edu/archives/CollectionsList/CollectionDescriptions/STtoUSArmy/unalaklt.wpd.html > (5/25/2005).

* University of Alaska Fairbanks. *Alaska Native Knowledge Network.* < http://www.ankn.uaf.edu/ > (5/25/2005).

Wohlforth, Charles. *Charles Wohlforth's Web Site.* < http://wohlforth.net/ > (5/25/2005).

Miscellaneous

Videos; unpublished dissertations, theses, and reports; newsletters; and personal letters and memoranda

Atkinson, F. H. D. "The Study of the Ovibos (Muskox) and the Possibilities of Ovibos Fibre from a Textile Standpoint." Thesis. Leeds, England: University of Leeds, 1922.

Bethel Broadcasting, Inc. *Cross on the Yukon.* VHS. Bethel, Alaska: Bethel Broadcasting, Inc., 1990.

Blakely, Dawn. "The Morphological, Physical, and Chemical Characteristics of Qiviut Fibre." Thesis. Toronto: University of Toronto, 1971.

Block, Sophia. Excerpts from personal letter sent to Musk Ox Project. February 1973.

Brooks, Maria. *The Reindeer Queen: Once the Richest Woman in Alaska—The True Story of Sinrock Mary.* DVD/VHS. Watertown, Massachusetts: Documentary Educational Resources, 2000.

Elder, Sarah, and Leonard Kamerling. *Tununeremiut: The People of Tununak.* DVD/VHS. Watertown, Massachusetts: Documentary Educational Resources, 1972.

Griffiths, Helen M. "Continuation of Report Written in Bethel to 23rd February, 1972." Memorandum, 1972.

———. "The Development of Qiviut." Manuscript for *Shuttle, Spindle and Dyepot,* April 24, 1975.

———. "Musk Ox Project." Unpublished report. University of Alaska, 1970.

———. "Report on Workshops Held 9th February, 1972 to Current Time, 23rd February." Memorandum, 1972.

Hott, Lawrence, Tom Litwin, and Diane Garey, producers. *The Harriman Alaska Expedition Retraced.* Haydenville, Massachusetts: Florentine Films/ Hott Productions, 2002.

———. "The Harriman Alaska Expedition Retraced Study Guide and Transcript." < http://www.florentinefilms.org/thefilms/16film.htm > (May 25, 2005).

Large Animal Research Station staff. "Muskoxen and Caribou Factoids." Fairbanks, Alaska, Large Animal Research Station, Institute of Arctic Biology, University of Alaska Fairbanks, n.d.

Musk Ox Farm. "Friends of the Musk Ox." Member Newsletter.

Musk Ox Project. "Musk Ox Project—Objective Statement: Utilization of Qiviut by an Eskimo Village." Unpublished Report. N.d. This report was located in the co-op library; the organization's name was the Musk Ox Project before the co-op was formed and incorporated.

Rutherford, John Gunion, James Stanley McLean, and James Dernard Harkin. Report of the Royal Comission: Appointed by Order in Council of date May 20th, 1919 to investigate the possibilities of the reindeer and musk-ox industries in the Arctic and sub-Arctic regions of Canada. Located at Dartmouth College in their special collections, in the papers of F. H. Atkinson. See < http://ead.dartmouth.edu/html/stem6.html > (7/19/2005).

Schell, Ann Lillian. Personal Letter to John J. Teal, Jr. February 1973.

Schell, Lillian Crowell. "The Musk Ox Underwool, Qiviut: Historical Uses and Present Utilization in an Eskimo Knitting Industry." Thesis. College, Alaska: University of Alaska Fairbanks, 1972.

Shell, Ann. "Report on Spinning, Knitting & Designing Workshop. Instructor: Dorothy Reade." Unpublished report. Eugene, Oregon, July 1968.

Teal, John J., Jr., Lillian C. Schell, and K. M. Rae. "The Establishment of an Arctic Village Industry Utilizing Qiviut, the Underwool of the Musk Ox." Report of the Musk Ox Project. N.d. (approx. 1970).

Wilkinson, Paul F., and Helen M. Griffiths. Untitled manuscript for Melliand Textil-Berichte. November 1974.

———. Untitled manuscript for Melliand Textil-Berichte. April 1975.

Name note: Ann Lillian Schell went by several different names, including Lillian Crowell, Lillian Crowell Shell, Ann Schell, and Ann Lillian Schell.

Index